CODEX™
SPACE MARINES®

BY ANDY CHAMBERS, JERVIS JOHNSON & GAVIN THORPE

Book Cover Art: David Gallagher

Internal Art: Alexander Boyd, Wayne England, Des Hanley,
Neil Hodgson, Nuala Kennedy, Paul Smith,
John Wigley & Richard Wright

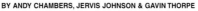

PRODUCED BY GAMES WORKSHOP

Citadel & the Citadel logo, Dark Angels, 'Eavy Metal, Games Workshop &
the Games Workshop logo, Space Marine and Warhammer are trademarks
of Games Workshop Ltd registered in the UK and elsewhere in the world.

Adeptus Astartes, Adeptus Mechanicus, Alpha Legion, Blood Angels, Blood Claws, Chimera,
Codex, Captain Cortez, Crimson Fists, Death Guard, Demolisher, Dreadnought,
Emperor's Champion, Emperor's Children, Fire Hawks, Imperial Fists, Iron Hands,
Iron Warriors, Land Raider, Land Speeder, Lunar Wolves, Lysander, Marneus Calgar, Night
Lords, Ork, Predator, Raven Guard, Razorback, Rhino, Salamanders,
Silver Skulls, Space Wolves, Tech-Priests, Terminator, Thousand Sons, Tigurius,
Thunderhawk, Tyranid, Ultramarines, Vindicator, Whirlwind, White Panthers, White Scars,
Word Bearers, Worldeaters and Xavier are all trademarks of Games Workshop Ltd.

British Cataloguing-in-Publication Data. A catalogue record
for this book is available from the British Library.

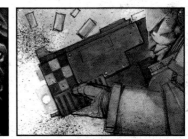

UK	US	AUSTRALIA	CANADA	HONG KONG
GAMES WORKSHOP LTD.	GAMES WORKSHOP INC.	GAMES WORKSHOP,	GAMES WORKSHOP,	GAMES WORKSHOP,
WILLOW RD,	6721 BAYMEADOW DRIVE,	23 LIVERPOOL ST,	1645 BONHILL RD,	2002-2006,
LENTON,	GLEN BURNIE,	INGLEBURN,	UNITS 9-11, MISSISSAUGA,	HORIZON PLAZA,
NOTTINGHAM	MARYLAND, 21060 6401	NSW 2565	TORONTO L5T 1R3	LEE WING ST,
NG7 2WS				AP LEI CHAU

GAMES WORKSHOP®

PRODUCT CODE: 60 03 01 01 002   Games Workshop World Wide Web site: http://www.games-workshop.com   ISBN: 1-869893-28-X

INTRODUCTION

> "Give me a hundred Space Marines. Or failing that give me a thousand other troops."
>
> Attributed to Rogal Dorn, Primarch of the Imperial Fists.

Welcome to Codex: Space Marines, a book entirely dedicated to collecting, painting and gaming with Space Marines in the Warhammer 40,000 battle game.

SPACE MARINES

Space Marines are the most powerful and dreaded of all the human warriors in Warhammer 40,000. They are not human at all but superhuman, having been made superior, in all respects, to a normal man by a harsh regime of genetic modification, psycho-conditioning and rigorous training. Being few in number compared to the uncounted billions of humanity, Space Marines are organised into small independent armies called Chapters. Each Chapter is responsible for its own recruitment, training, equipment, organisation and strategy. Their unswerving loyalty is to the Emperor of Mankind and no other.

WHY COLLECT A SPACE MARINE ARMY

Space Marines are without doubt one of the best armies available in Warhammer 40,000, especially for first-time collectors. Why? Because they are as hard as nails! Even the most basic Space Marine trooper is a formidable model in the Warhammer 40,000 game.

A Space Marine's characteristics equal or better those of the elite troops of other forces, combining both excellent hand-to-hand weapon skills and shooting accuracy with high Strength and Toughness values. They also benefit from a good Initiative value and a zealous determination to never give way before the scum-sucking alien foes of humanity.

Space Marines are also armed and armoured as befits an elite fighting force. They are equipped for battle with a wide selection of deadly weaponry ranging from the boltgun up to the deadly assault cannon and Whirlwind multi-launchers. Best of all is their superb power armour, which in itself means that two thirds of the wounds they would suffer in combat will simply bounce off.

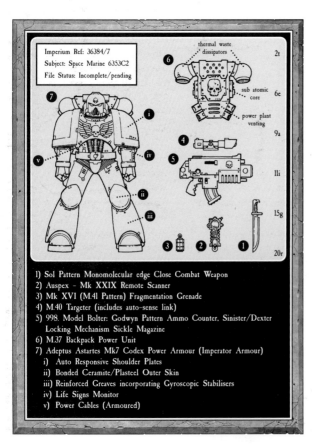

Imperium Ref: 36384/7
Subject: Space Marine 6353C2
File Status: Incomplete/pending

thermal waste dissipators

sub atomic core

power plant venting

1) Sol Pattern Monomolecular edge Close Combat Weapon
2) Auspex - Mk XXIX Remote Scanner
3) Mk XVI (M.41 Pattern) Fragmentation Grenade
4) M.40 Targeter (includes auto-sense link)
5) 998. Model Bolter: Godwyn Pattern Ammo Counter, Sinister/Dexter Locking Mechanism Sickle Magazine
6) M.37 Backpack Power Unit
7) Adeptus Astartes Mk7 Codex Power Armour (Imperator Armour)
   i) Auto Responsive Shoulder Plates
   ii) Bonded Ceramite/Plasteel Outer Skin
   iii) Reinforced Greaves incorporating Gyroscopic Stabilisers
   iv) Life Signs Monitor
   v) Power Cables (Armoured)

Space Marines also offer a number of advantages in terms of collecting an army. A Space Marine force is compact and efficient so a relatively small number of models are needed to field a battleworthy army. This makes Space Marines easy on the pocket and quick to paint up ready for action.

The colour schemes for many of the Space Marine Chapters are very simple to paint, or you could come up with your own Chapter colours. Adding extra detail to your models is just as easy to do because there is a wide selection of waterslide transfer sheets and self adhesive banners readily available for those of us who are all fingers and thumbs when it comes to doing detail work.

"While vile mutants still draw breath, there can be no peace. While obscene heretics' hearts still beat, there can be no respite. While faithless traitors still live, there can be no forgiveness."

Legiones Astartes Silver Skulls' Catechism of Hate,
Verse I of XXV

TRANSMITTED:	Kethra
RECEIVED:	IQ-0XX
DESTINATION:	IQ-0III
TELEPATHIC DUCT:	Astropath-terminus Jessiah

+ + + + + + + + + DATE: 7335332.M39
+ + + + + + + + + + REF: Inq/0ii59704311/GT
+ + + + + + + + + + + BY: Inquisitor Grim
+ + + + + + + + + + + RE: Legions Astartes Heretic Suppression
+ + + + + + + THOUGHT: Seek reward in service alone.

Honoured masters, my recent investigations on Kethra uncovered nothing less than a worldwide conspiracy to secede from the Emperor's Light and the guiding rule of the Imperium. The situation was dire as the conspiracy originated from the Governor himself, and was supported by his most prominent ministers and officers. Under the circumstances my only option was to transmit a general appeal for assistance and wait for help to arrive. My petition was soon answered by Space Marines of the White Panthers Chapter. Upon their arrival in the Kethra system, I advised them of the situation and outlined my plan to eliminate the Governor and his advisory council, also targeting the high-ranking officers of the defence force. They thanked me for bringing this heresy to their attention and proceeded to implement their own plan.

The first attack destroyed Kethra's two orbiting weapon stations, with a crew of nearly 15,000 men. Having established orbital supremacy, they despatched Thunderhawks and drop pods to various points on the planet's surface, calculated to provoke an attack by the Kethran defence forces. Despite their vast advantage in numbers the attacking forces were annihilated piecemeal by the White Panthers over a period of a few days and nights of incessant conflict. I found it regrettable that the common soldiers bore the weight of the Space Marine's fury, as they were merely men following orders and their chain of command as they had been so trained to do; it was their leaders who required justice. But to a Space Marine, one of the Emperor's finest, there is never an excuse for such heresy, each man must owe loyalty to the Emperor before any other.

Having shattered the defence force, the White Panthers launched an all-out assault on the Governor's Palace. Surrounded, the Governor's men had little choice but to grimly fight to the death. A few managed to flee, but noone else survived. The Governor and his consulate were summarily executed as traitors, and demolition charges were used to destroy the planet's armoury. Having deemed their missions achieved, with Kethra's military power eliminated, the White Panthers returned to their battle barge and left without further word.

Whether Kethra will be sufficiently recovered to provide its tithe within the next year is a matter for the Administratum. The point I wish to raise is that the proper application of force could have resolved the entire affair without destroying the military strength of Kethra and leaving the world vulnerable to alien attack. I regret that

the Officio Assassinorum did not respond to my request earlier when their Adepts could have easily ended the whole affair quickly and quietly.

While the warriors of the Adeptus Astartes, as ever, showed creditable skill, determination and unswerving loyalty to the Emperor, unleashing them against any Imperial world is to use an ultimate force exceeded only by that of Exterminatus. It is not as if this incident is without precedent, indeed on many occasions Space Marines have pursued their own campaigns without reference or remit to the authority of the Adeptus Terra. To think that there are a thousand Chapters, each a thousand-strong, of these warriors poised to strike anywhere in the galaxy fills me with reassurance and dread in equal measure.

I remain, as ever, you most faithful and obedient servant,
Inquisitor Bastalek Grim

WHAT'S IN THIS BOOK

This book breaks down into the three main sections. Each section describes a different area of creating your own Space Marine force and getting it into action on the tabletop battlefield.

The Army List. Tells you about the different characters, troops, weapons and vehicles available to a Space Marine force, and how to work out an army for use in a Warhammer 40,000 game.

Painting and Collecting Guide. Describes choosing an army, basic tactics plus step-by-step details of assembling and painting models and vehicles. This section also shows examples of Space Marine colour schemes and markings, gives advice on creating your own schemes and tips on modelling and converting.

The Appendix. The final section is dedicated to background details and extra information about Space Marines.

"Advance!" The order rang across the comm-net like a clarion call. The battle brethren surged forward without hesitation, bolters roaring as their bullets battered at the ruined farm ahead. Return fire from the Orks lashed at the Space Marines. Tracer fire and screaming shells filled the air, ricocheting off their armour and forcing them to struggle forward as if into the teeth of a storm. But the farm had to be captured, the Orks' big guns had to be silenced.

Brother Beliasus was struck square in the chest. Flecks of melted ceramite sprayed across his face plate and icons across his helmet display flickered warning orange as his armour struggled to keep him upright. It failed and he went down on one knee. Not two yards away Brother Eveay fell with two fist-sized holes through his abdomen, his bright blood mixing with the dark earth. At that instant the heavy weapons of the Devastators spoke with one voice and the perimeter buildings were rent by fiery explosions. Almost immediately the Orks' firing slackened to sporadic bursts.

Beliasus heaved himself upright, the armour's musculature grinding as it tried to keep up with his movements. Icons were still flashing as he levelled his bolter and blasted at a figure silhouetted in a ruined window. The greenskin disappeared under the hail of explosive bolts and Beliasus boosted the power to his legs to lope forward and regain his place in the battleline.

His armour hadn't been the same since the insurrection on Lannis IX five years ago. The armour had never truly recovered its spirit since the injury and the replacement parts were weaker and slower than the old ones. The Tech-Priests had lost so much knowledge, they simply didn't make things like they used to. He banished the heretical thought in an instant. "Never doubt the righteousness of Man," Brother Mortez had told them. "Though you have been elevated by the blessings of the Emperor you are still the servants of Man. It is doubt that forms the path to damnation."

Beliasus caught up with Brother Julo and Brother Varas as they prepared to assault the outer wall. Julo's armour was scarred in a dozen different places where he had been hit but he calmly slammed another clip into his boltgun as if at morning firing rites. Varas gave the signal and they stormed through a breach together. To their left and right more armoured brethren burst through the perimeter walls.

A horde of Orks spilled out of the shattered buildings like a green tide, beyond them their crude artillery unleashed another salvo. At such close range it was devastating, fire and smoke exploded all about and Beliasus felt his helm ring like a bell as red-hot shrapnel ricocheted off it. Julo fell with a curse, his arm torn away at the elbow. Yells and gunshots filled the air as the Orks closed in on the battered Space Marines. Beliasus and the others took up firing stances and pumped bolter shots into the oncoming horde. Even Julo managed to heft his bolter in his remaining hand and open fire. Every shot punched another howling Ork off its feet but they raced forward oblivious to casualties, bloodlust twisting their bestial faces. The remaining brethren were so outnumbered that they would likely be swept away by their onslaught.

Then it happened. A section of wall collapsed inward and a massive, hulking form crunched in over the rubble. It stood twice the height of a man and was so bulky and heavily armoured that it looked more like a walking tank than an armoured suit. Without breaking stride it raised the multi-barrelled cannon set into the angled armour plates of its arm and opened fire on the Orks. Explosions ripped through their ranks like a scythe. With joy Brother Beliasus recognised the ancient heraldry which the Dreadnought displayed, and charged forward to follow the venerable Brother Mortez into the heart of the Ork horde.

SPACE MARINE ARMY LIST

The army list and all other information in the Space Marines Codex takes precedence over the Space Marines army list that is in the Warhammer 40,000 rulebook. On the following pages you will find an army list which will allow you to field a Space Marine army in games of Warhammer 40,000. The Space Marine army list not only allows you to fight battles using the scenarios included in the Warhammer 40,000 rulebook, but it also provides you with the basic information you'll require in order to field a Space Marine army in scenarios that you have devised yourself, or that form part of a campaign you are playing in.

The army list is split into five distinct sections: *Headquarters (HQ)*, *Elites*, *Troops*, *Fast Attack* and *Heavy Assault*. All of the squads, vehicles and characters in an army list are placed in one of the five sections depending upon their role on the battlefield. In addition, every model included in the army list is given a points value, which varies depending upon how effective that model is in combat. Before you can choose an army for a game you will need to agree with your opponent upon a scenario and the total number of points each of you will spend on your army. Having done this you can proceed to pick an army using the following guidelines.

FORCE ORGANISATION CHARTS

The army lists are used in conjunction with the force organisation charts from a scenario. Each chart is split into five categories that correspond to the sections in the army list, and each category may have one or more boxes. Each box indicates that you *may make one choice* from that section of the army list, while a dark-toned box means that you *must make a choice* from that section.

Note that unless a model or vehicle forms part of a squad or a squadron, it counts as a single choice from those available to your army.

USING THE ARMY LISTS

To choose units you need to look in the relevant section of the army list and decide what character, unit or vehicle you want, how many models will be in the unit, and what upgrades you want (if any). Remember, you cannot field models equipped with weapons and wargear not shown on the model. Once this is done subtract its cost from your army's total points, and then go back and make another choice. Continue this until you have spent all your points. Then find a big bucket of dice, and get ready to destroy the enemies of Mankind.

ARMY LIST ENTRIES

Each army list entry consists of the following:

Unit Name: The type of unit and any limitations (if any) on the maximum number of choices you can make for it (eg 0-1).

Profile: These are the characteristics of that unit type, including its points cost. Where the unit has different warriors, there may be more than one profile.

Number/Squad: The number of models allowed in the unit, or the number of models you may take for one choice from the force organisation chart. Often this is a variable amount, in which case it shows the minimum and maximum unit size.

Weapons: These are the unit's standard weapons.

Options: Lists the different weapon/equipment options for the unit and any additional points cost for taking them. It may also include the option to upgrade a squad member to a character. If a squad is allowed to have models with upgraded weaponry (ie heavy weapons, plasma guns, etc) then these may only be taken by ordinary squad members, not the Sergeant.

Special Rules: This is where you'll find any special rules that apply to the unit.

STANDARD MISSIONS

COMPULSORY
1 HQ
2 Troops

OPTIONAL
1 HQ
4 Troops
3 Elites
3 Fast Attack
3 Heavy Support

The Standard Missions force organisation chart is a good example of how to choose an army. To begin with you will need at least one HQ unit and two Troop units (dark shaded boxes indicate units that __must__ be taken for the mission). This leaves the following for you to choose from to make up your army's total points value: up to 1 HQ unit, 0-3 additional Elite units, 0-4 additional Troop units, 0-3 additional Fast Attack units or 0-3 additional Heavy Support units.

SPECIAL RULES

'And They Shall Know no Fear'
Space Marines automatically regroup as they fall back, even if the squad is reduced to less than 50% by casualties. If the enemy advance into them the Space Marines are not destroyed and the advancement of the enemy unit is treated as a new assault (enemy striking: +1A the following turn) in the same way as a sweeping advance. If the enemy do not advance into them the Space Marines are free to move, shoot and assault normally in their following turn.

Drop Pods
At the start of a battle where you can use the *Deep Strike* rules, you can declare that your Space Marines are deploying by landing in drop pods from orbiting spacecraft. Models doing this deploy using the *Deep Strike* rules in the Warhammer 40,000 rulebook.

Only the following can deploy from drop pods. No other models in the army can be used in this mission (they stay onboard ship).

- *Any Space Marine model in power or Terminator armour*
- *Space Marine Scouts*
- *Dreadnoughts and Land Speeders*

SPACE MARINE ARMOURY

Characters can have up to two single-handed weapons, or a single-handed weapon and a two-handed weapon. You may also pick 100 points worth of wargear per model but no model may be given the same item twice. Models wearing Terminator armour can only use wargear and weapons marked with a '*'. The full rules for Space Marine wargear can be found on pages 34-35. All wargear and weapons must be represented on the model.

SINGLE-HANDED WEAPONS

Bolt pistol . . . . 1 pt
Chainfist (Terminators only) . . . . 30 pts*
Close combat weapon. . . . . 1 pt
Force weapon (Librarians only) . . . . 40 pts*
Lightning Claw (single) 25pts*
Lightning Claw (pair, count as two choices) 30pts*
Plasma pistol. . . . . 15 pts
Power fist. . . . . 25 pts*
Power weapon . . . . 15 pts*
Storm Shield[1] . . . . 10 pts*
Thunder Hammer. . . . . 30 pts*

TWO-HANDED WEAPONS

Bolter . . . . 2 pts
Combi-weapons:
    Bolter-flamer . . . . 10 pts*
    Bolter-grenade launcher. . . . . 10 pts*
    Bolter-plasma gun . . . . 15 pts*
    Bolter-meltagun. . . . . 15 pts*
Storm bolter. . . . . 5 pts*

VEHICLE UPGRADES

Some vehicles can have the following equipment upgrades. The upgrades that may be taken are listed in the entry for the vehicle in the army list. All upgrades must be shown on the model and no upgrade can be taken more than once.

Dozer blade. . . . . 5 pts
Extra armour. . . . . 5 pts
Hunter-killer missile . . . . 15 pts
Pintle-mounted storm bolter. . . . . 10 pts
Searchlight . . . . 1 pt
Smoke launchers . . . . 3 pts

WARGEAR

Artificer armour (independent characters only[2]). . . . . 20 pts
Auspex . . . . 2 pts*
Bionics . . . . 10 pts
Chapter banner (Standard Bearer only[3]). . . . . 60 pts*
Frag grenades . . . . 1 pt
Holy relic (Standard Bearer or Chaplain only,
          no more than one per army[3]) . . . . . . 40 pts*
Iron Halo (one per army). . . . . 25 pts
Jump pack (independent characters only[2]). . . . . 20 pts
Krak grenades . . . . 2 pts
Narthecium (Apothecaries only) . . . . 25 pts
Master-crafted weapon 15pts*
Melta bombs. . . . . 5 pts
Psychic hood (Librarians only) . . . . 25 pts*
Purity seals . . . . 5 pts*
Reductor (Apothecaries only) . . . . 5 pts
Sacred standard (standard bearer only) . . . . . . 20 pts
Servo-arm (Techmarines only) . . . . 30 pts
Signum (Techmarines only). . . . . 15 pts
Space Marine bike (independent characters only[2]) . . 35 pts
Teleport homer . . . . 5 pts*
Terminator armour (Does not include weapons,
         independent characters only[2]) . . . 25 pts
Terminator honours. . . . . 15 pts

Notes

1) *Although a storm shield is not a weapon as such, it counts as a single-handed weapon because nothing else can be used by the arm holding the shield.*

2) *Note that Veteran Sergeants, Apothecaries, Techmarines and standard bearers are not independent characters.*

3) *Only armies of 2,000 points or more may take a Chapter banner, and only armies of 3,000 points or more may have a Chapter banner and a holy relic.*

"With the bolter, cleanse the unclean.
We will cleanse!
―
With the flamer, purify the unholy.
We will purify!
―
With the chainsword, purge the corrupt.
We will purge!
―
With the missile, kill the impure.
We will kill!"

HQ

SPACE MARINE HEROES

	Points	WS	BS	S	T	W	I	A	Ld	Sv
Leader	30	4	4	4	4	1	4	2	9	3+
Commander	45	5	5	4	4	2	5	3	9	3+
Force Commander	60	5	5	4	4	3	5	3	10	3+

Options: The Hero can be given any equipment allowed from the Space Marine Armoury.

SPECIAL RULES

Independent Character: Unless accompanied by a Command squad, a Hero is an independent character and follows the Independent Character special rules in the Warhammer 40,000 rulebook.

Command Squad: The Hero may be accompanied by a Command squad, see the Command squad entry for details. Note that the Hero and the Command squad count as a single HQ choice.

Depending upon its size and the importance of its mission, a Space Marine force may be led by an experienced veteran, a Company Captain, or even the Chapter Master himself.

LIBRARIAN

	Points	WS	BS	S	T	W	I	A	Ld	Sv
Librarian	60	5	5	4	4	2	5	3	9	3+

Options: The Librarian can be given any equipment allowed from the Space Marine Armoury.

SPECIAL RULES

Independent Character: Unless accompanied by a Command squad, a Librarian is an independent character and follows the Independent Character special rules in the Warhammer 40,000 rulebook.

Psychic Power – Smite: The Librarian can attempt to *Smite* his enemy in his own shooting phase. *Smite* counts as a weapon and hits automatically using the following profile:

Range 12"	Strength 4	AP 2	Assault 1/Blast

Command Squad: The Librarian may be accompanied by a Command squad, see the Command squad entry for details. Note that the Librarian and the Command squad count as a single HQ choice.

Librarians use their psychic powers to unleash devastating attacks, as well as augmenting their own physical prowess.

LIBRARIANS

Space Marine Librarians can make a special psychic attack against enemy models. The rules for using psychic powers can be found on page 74 of the Warhammer 40,000 rulebook.

CHAPLAIN

	Points	WS	BS	S	T	W	I	A	Ld	Sv
Chaplain	70	5	5	4	4	2	5	3	9	3+

Weapons: Crozius arcanum and rosarius (cost of wargear included in Chaplain's points value).

Options: The Chaplain can be given any equipment allowed from the Space Marine Armoury.

SPECIAL RULES

Independent Character: Unless accompanied by a Command squad, a Chaplain is an independent character and follows the Independent Character special rules in the Warhammer 40,000 rulebook.

Command Squad: The Chaplain may be accompanied by a Command squad, see the Command squad entry for details. Note that the Chaplain and the Command squad count as a single HQ choice.

Chaplains attend to the spiritual well being of their battle brothers. They are often found in the thickest of the fighting, exhorting their comrades to even greater acts of bravery.

It is usual for noted Space Marine warriors to be accompanied by a cadre of highly disciplined veterans. A Command squad often includes honoured warriors such as a standard bearer, Apothecary or Techmarine.

COMMAND SQUAD

	Points/Model	WS	BS	S	T	W	I	A	Ld	Sv
Bodyguard	18	4	4	4	4	1	4	1	9	3+
Veteran Sergeant	+12	4	4	4	4	1	4	2	9	3+

You may take a Command squad to accompany any other HQ unit in your army. See the other HQ entries on the previous page for details.

Squad: The Bodyguard consists of one Space Marine Sergeant and between four and nine Space Marines.

Weapons: Bolter. The Sergeant can exchange his bolter for a bolt pistol and close combat weapon at no extra points cost.

Options: Up to two Space Marines in the squad can have: missile launcher at +20 pts; heavy bolter at +15 pts; lascannon at +35 pts; flamer at +3 pts; plasma gun at +6 pts; meltagun at +10 pts. The entire squad can have frag grenades at an additional cost of +1 pt per model and krak grenades at an additional cost of +2 pts per model.

CHARACTERS

One model can be upgraded to an Apothecary, one model can be upgraded to a Techmarine, and one model can be upgraded to a Standard Bearer. Any of these can take equipment from the Space Marine Armoury. The Sergeant can be upgraded to Veteran Sergeant at an additional cost of +12 pts.

Terminator Honours: If the squad is led by either a Hero, Librarian or Chaplain with Terminator honours and already has a Veteran Sergeant then the rest of the squad may have Terminator honours at an additional cost of +10 pts per model.

Transport Vehicle: The entire squad may be mounted in a Rhino at an additional cost of +50 pts, a Razorback at an additional cost of +70 pts, or a Land Raider at an additional cost of +250 pts (see appropriate vehicle entry for upgrade options).

ELITES

Terminators are the most feared of all Space Marine warriors. They combine centuries of experience with the best armour and weapons that can be found in the Imperium. Terminators often spearhead the Space Marines' attacks, blowing apart the enemy at range, before crushing them in a final, ruthless assault.

TERMINATOR SQUAD

	Points/Model	WS	BS	S	T	W	I	A	Ld	Sv
Terminator	42	4	4	4	4	1	4	2	9	2+

Squad: The squad consists of one Space Marine Terminator Sergeant and between four and nine Space Marine Terminators. The +1 Attack bonus for having Terminator honours and the Terminator armour's 2+ save have already been included in the characteristics above.

Weapons: The Terminator Sergeant is equipped with a power sword and storm bolter. The Space Marine Terminators are armed with power fists and storm bolters.

Options: Any model may replace its power fist with a chainfist for +5 pts. Up to two models may be armed with one of the following weapons: assault cannon at +20 pts; heavy flamer at +10 pts; Cyclone missile launcher at +20 pts. The Cyclone missile launcher replaces the model's power fist, and the other weapons replace its storm bolter.

The Terminator Sergeant may have additional equipment from the Space Marine Armoury.

SPECIAL RULES

Deep Strike: Space Marine models with Terminator armour may *Deep Strike*. See the Terminator Armour rules in the Wargear section.

TERMINATOR ASSAULT SQUAD

	Points/Model	WS	BS	S	T	W	I	A	Ld	Sv
Terminator	42	4	4	4	4	1	4	2	9	2+

Squad: The squad consists of one Space Marine Sergeant and between four and nine Space Marine Terminators. The Terminator armour's 2+ save and +1 Attack bonus have already been included in the characteristics above.

Weapons: The Sergeant is armed with a storm bolter and a power sword. All models in the squad are armed with either a pair of lightning claws or a thunder hammer and storm shield.

Options: Any number of Terminators may swap their close combat weapons for a storm bolter and power fist at no additional cost. The power fist may be upgraded to a chainfist at +5 pts.

The Terminator Sergeant may be given additional equipment from the Space Marine Armoury.

SPECIAL RULES

Deep Strike: Space Marine models with Terminator armour may *Deep Strike*. See the Terminator Armour rules in the Wargear section.

Terminators equipped with specialist close combat weaponry such as lightning claws and thunder hammers are used in dense fighting conditions, such as spaceship boarding actions, or in the depths of a hive city.

DREADNOUGHT

	Points/Model	WS	BS	S	Armour: Front	Armour: Side	Armour: Rear	I	A
Dreadnought	75	4	4	6(10)	12	12	10	4	2

Type: Walker   **Crew:** One Space Marine

Weapons: The Dreadnought's left arm is equipped with a Dreadnought close combat weapon that has a built-in storm bolter. The Dreadnought's right arm is equipped with one weapon from the following list: assault cannon at +30 pts; twin-linked lascannon at +50 pts; twin-linked heavy bolter at +30 pts; multi-melta at +40 pts, plasma cannon at +40 pts; twin-linked autocannon at +35 pts.

Options: The Dreadnought may be equipped with any of the following vehicle upgrades for the cost listed in the Space Marine Armoury: extra armour, searchlight or smoke launchers. No upgrade may be chosen more than once per Dreadnought.

The storm bolter may be upgraded to a heavy flamer at an additional cost of +10 pts.

The Dreadnought's close combat weapon can be upgrade to a missile launcher at an additional cost of +10 pts.

A Dreadnought is piloted by a mighty Space Marine warrior who has been saved from death by his internment within its armoured sarcophagus. In this way the warrior can continue to vanquish the foes of the Emperor for many centuries, or even millennia.

SPACE MARINE VETERAN SQUAD

	Points/Model	WS	BS	S	T	W	I	A	Ld	Sv
Veteran Space Marine	18	4	4	4	4	1	4	1	9	3+
Veteran Sergeant	+12	4	4	4	4	1	4	2	9	3+

Squad: The squad consists of between five and ten Veteran Space Marines.

Weapons: Bolter or bolt pistol and close combat weapon.

Options: One Space Marine may have one of the following: heavy bolter at +5 pts; missile launcher at +10 pts; lascannon at +15 pts. In addition, one Space Marine may be armed with one of the following: flamer at +6 pts; meltagun at +10 pts; plasma gun at +6 pts.

The entire squad may be given frag grenades at an additional cost of +1 pt per model and krak grenades at an additional cost of +2 pts per model. One Veteran Space Marine can be upgraded to Veteran Sergeant at an additional cost of +12 pts.

Terminator Honours: If the squad is led by a Veteran Sergeant, then the rest of the squad may have Terminator honours at an additional cost of +10 pts per model.

Transport Vehicle: The entire squad may be mounted in a Rhino at an additional cost of +50 pts or a Razorback at an additional cost of +70 pts (see Transport entry for upgrade options).

Exceptional warriors amongst the Space Marines are inducted into the prestigious First Company, where they receive additional training in all aspects of warcraft. Many learn how to use the dreaded Terminator suits, while others excel at other forms of fighting. All are equipped to the highest standard, and they are most often seen at the forefront of the fighting.

TROOPS

Tactical squads form the mainstay of each Space Marine Chapter. They are versatile fighters, able to speed forward in a Rhino and fight the enemy in close combat, or stay back and give supporting fire with their heavy weapons. It is the Tactical squads' ability to fulfil a number of widely differing roles that makes the Space Marines so effective, whatever combat situation they find themselves in.

Scout Squads are experts at fighting independently from the main force. They strike deep into enemy territory, destroying supplies and the enemy's communications with their commando raids.

SPACE MARINE TACTICAL SQUAD

	Points/Model	WS	BS	S	T	W	I	A	Ld	Sv
Space Marine	15	4	4	4	4	1	4	1	8	3+
Veteran Sergeant	+15	4	4	4	4	1	4	2	9	3+

Squad: The squad consists of one Space Marine Sergeant and between four and nine Space Marines.

Weapons: Bolters. The Sergeant may replace his bolter with a bolt pistol and close combat weapon at no extra points cost.

Options: One Space Marine in the squad may be armed with one of the following weapons: heavy bolter at +5 pts; missile launcher at +10 pts; or a lascannon at +15 pts.

In addition one Space Marine in the squad may be armed with one of the following weapons: flamer at +6 pts; meltagun at +10 pts; plasma gun at +6 pts.

The entire squad may be given frag grenades at an additional cost of +1 pt per model and krak grenades at an additional cost of +2 pts per model.

The Sergeant may be upgraded to a Veteran Sergeant at an additional cost of +15 pts.

Transport Vehicle: The entire squad may be mounted in a Rhino at an extra cost of +50 pts or a Razorback at an extra cost of +70 pts (see Transport entry for upgrade options).

SCOUT SQUAD

	Points/Model	WS	BS	S	T	W	I	A	Ld	Sv
Scout	13	4	4	4	4	1	4	1	8	4+
Scout Sergeant	13	4	4	4	4	1	4	1	8	4+
Veteran Scout Sergeant	+13	4	4	4	4	1	4	2	9	4+

Squad: The Scout squad consists of one Space Marine Scout Sergeant and between four and nine Space Marine Scouts.

Weapons. Bolt pistol and close combat weapon.

Options: Any model in the squad may replace their bolt pistol and close combat weapon with a sniper rifle at +5 pts, or a bolter or shotgun at no additional points cost.

Up to one model in the squad may be armed with one of the following weapons: heavy bolter at +15pts; autocannon at +20pts; missile launcher at +20pts.

The entire squad may be equipped with frag grenades at an additional cost of +1 pt per model and krak grenades at an additional cost of +2 pts. The Scout Sergeant can be upgraded to a Veteran Scout Sergeant at an additional cost of +13 pts.

SPECIAL RULES

Infiltrators: In the right circumstances Scouts can work their way into a forward position on the battlefield. To represent this they may set up using the *Infiltrators* rule, but only if the mission allows *Infiltrators*. If it does not then they set up normally with the rest of the army.

Move Through Cover: Scouts roll an extra D6 when rolling to move through difficult terrain. In most cases this will mean that they roll 3D6 and pick the dice with the highest score.

Transport: RHINO

	Points	Front Armour	Side Armour	Rear Armour	BS
Rhino	50	11	11	10	4

Type: Tank   **Crew:** Space Marines

Weapons: The Rhino is armed with a storm bolter.

Options: The Rhino may be equipped with any of the following vehicle upgrades for the cost listed in the Space Marine Armoury: dozer blades, extra armour, hunter-killer missile, pintle-mounted storm bolter, searchlight, smoke launchers. No upgrade may be chosen more than once per vehicle.

Transport: The Rhino can carry up to ten Space Marines but may not carry Terminators.

Transport: RAZORBACK

	Points	Front Armour	Side Armour	Rear Armour	BS
Razorback	70	11	11	10	4

Type: Tank.   **Crew:** Space Marines

Weapons: The Razorback turret is armed with twin-linked heavy bolters.

Options: The twin-linked heavy bolters may be upgraded to one of the following: twin-linked lascannon +20 pts; multi-melta +5 pts; lascannon and twin-linked plasma guns +15 pts. The Razorback can have any of the following vehicle upgrades at the cost given in the Space Marine Armoury: dozer blades, extra armour, hunter-killer missile, pintle-mounted storm bolter, searchlight or smoke launchers. No upgrade can be used more than once per vehicle.

Transport: The Razorback can carry up to six Space Marines but may not carry Terminators.

TRANSPORTING TROOPS

Certain Space Marine squads (as indicated in their army list entry) can use Rhinos and Razorbacks to move rapidly across a battlefield. Neither vehicle counts as part of a squad or use up any choices on the force organisation chart.

The Rhino allows the Space Marines to move swiftly to seize an objective or strike deep into the heart of an enemy force.

The Razorback combines solid firepower with a modest troop-carrying capacity. While its guns blaze, it speeds into position to deploy a combat squad into the heart of the enemy army.

The enemies of the Emperor fear many things.

They fear discovery, defeat, despair and death.

Yet there is one thing they fear above all others.

They fear the wrath of the Space Marines!

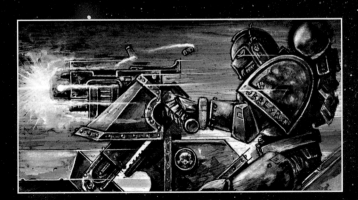

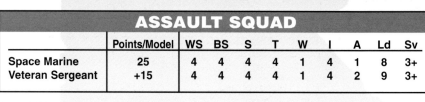

FAST ATTACK

ASSAULT SQUAD

	Points/Model	WS	BS	S	T	W	I	A	Ld	Sv
Space Marine	25	4	4	4	4	1	4	1	8	3+
Veteran Sergeant	+15	4	4	4	4	1	4	2	9	3+

Squad: The squad consists of one Space Marine Sergeant and between four and nine Space Marines.

Weapons: Bolt pistol, close combat weapons and frag grenades. The whole squad is equipped with jump packs.

Options: The entire squad can be equipped with krak grenades at +2 pts per model and/or melta bombs at +4 pts per model. Up to two models per squad can be equipped with plasma pistols at +5 pts each.

Character: The Sergeant of the Assault squad may be upgraded to a Veteran Sergeant for a cost of +15 pts. The Veteran Sergeant may be given additional equipment from the Space Marine Armoury.

SPECIAL RULES

Remove Jump Packs: Space Marine Assault squads can fight without jump packs if desired. If they do so then the cost of each model is reduced to 15 pts.

Deep Strike: Space Marine models with jump packs may *Deep Strike*. See the Jump Pack rules in the Wargear section.

> **X** Assault squads strike hard and fast. Their jump packs allow them to rapidly close with the enemy, and there are few adversaries who can withstand them once they are caught in bloody mêlée.

BIKE SQUADRON

	Points/Model	WS	BS	S	T	W	I	A	Ld	Sv
Space Marine Biker	35	4	4	4	4(5)	1	4	1	8	3+
Veteran Sergeant	+15	4	4	4	4(5)	1	4	2	9	3+
Attack Bike	50	4	4	4	4(5)	1	4	2	8	2+

Squad: The squadron consists of one Space Marine Sergeant and between two to four Space Marines riding bikes.

Weapons: Each bike is fitted with twin-linked bolters. Each Space Marine biker is armed with a bolt pistol.

Options: Up two Space Marines in the squad may be armed with one of the following weapons: flamer at +3 pts; meltagun at +10 pts; plasma gun at +6 pts.

The Sergeant may be armed with a close combat weapon at +1 pt.

The Sergeant may be upgraded to a Veteran Sergeant at an additional cost of +15 pts.

Attack Bike: The bike squadron may include one attack bike at a cost of 50 pts. The attack bike is armed with a heavy bolter. The heavy bolter may be replaced with a multi-melta for an additional cost of +15 points.

> **X** Bike squadrons are often used for reconnaissance missions into enemy held territory. When part of a larger battleforce, their speed and hitting power gives the Space Marine commander a fast, hard-hitting punch to his attack.

> **X** Attack bikes often accompany bike squads to provide heavy weapons support. When fielded as squadrons, they are highly mobile units with enough firepower to destroy even the largest enemy units, or blow apart tanks with their short-ranged multi-meltas.

ATTACK BIKE SQUADRON

	Points/Model	WS	BS	S	T	W	I	A	Ld	Sv
Attack Bike	50	4	4	4	4(5)	1	4	2	8	2+

Squad: The squadron consists of between one and three Space Marine attack bikes.

Weapons: Each bike is fitted with twin-linked bolters and a pintle-mounted heavy bolter. Each Space Marine rider is armed with a bolt pistol.

Options: Each attack bike can replace its heavy bolter with a multi-melta for +15 pts.

SCOUT BIKE SQUADRON

	Points/Model	WS	BS	S	T	W	I	A	Ld	Sv
Scout Biker	30	4	4	4	4(5)	1	4	1	8	4+
Scout Sergeant	30	4	4	4	4(5)	1	4	1	8	4+
Veteran Scout Sergeant	+15	4	4	4	4(5)	1	4	2	9	4+

Squad: The squadron consists of one Space Marine Scout Sergeant and between two to four Space Marine Scouts riding Space Marine bikes.

Weapons: Each bike has twin-linked bolters and each Scout is armed with a bolt pistol.

Options: Any model in the squad can replace their bolt pistol with a bolter or combat shotgun at no extra cost. The Scout Sergeant can have a close combat weapon for +1 pt. The whole squad may have frag grenades at an extra cost of +1 pt per model and krak grenades at an extra cost of +2 pts per model. The Scout Sergeant can be upgraded to a Veteran Scout Sergeant at an extra cost of +15 pts.

SPECIAL RULES

Difficult Terrain: Scout bikes may re-roll a failed Difficult Terrain test.

LAND SPEEDER SQUADRON

	Points/model	Front Armour	Side Armour	Rear Armour	BS
Land Speeder	50	10	10	10	4

Squad: Land speeders are fielded in squadrons of between one to three vehicles.

Type: Fast, Skimmer. Note that as the crew of a land speeder are wearing power armour, the land speeder does not count as open-topped.

Crew: Space Marines.

Weapons: Heavy bolter.

Options: The heavy bolter can be upgraded to a multi-melta at an additional cost of +15 pts.

LAND SPEEDER TORNADO

	Points	Front Armour	Side Armour	Rear Armour	BS
Tornado	75	10	10	10	4

Type: Fast, Skimmer. Note that as the crew of a land speeder are wearing power armour the land speeder does not count as open-topped.

Crew: Space Marines

Weapons: Heavy bolter plus a heavy flamer.

Options: The heavy bolter may be upgraded to a multi-melta at an additional cost of +15 pts, and the heavy flamer may be upgraded to an assault cannon at an additional cost of +10 pts.

LAND SPEEDER TYPHOON

	Points	Front Armour	Side Armour	Rear Armour	BS
Typhoon	75	10	10	10	4

Type: Fast, Skimmer. Note that as the crew of a land speeder are wearing power armour the land speeder does not count as open-topped.

Crew: Space Marines.

Weapons: Heavy bolter plus a twin-linked Typhoon missile launcher (see Weapons Summary on page 15 for Typhoon missile profile).

Options: The heavy bolter may be upgraded to a multi-melta at an additional cost of +15 pts.

✕ The Tenth Company of many Space Marine Chapters maintains a force of bikes. Some are employed to train new recruits who will eventually join bike squadrons as full battle brothers, others are used to provide highly mobile support for Scout squads behind enemy lines.

✕ The Space Marine land speeder is renowned for its high speed and mobility. Able to bring its heavy weapon to bear against almost anything on the battlefield, they are often employed to cut down enemy heavy weapons teams in cover or, when upgraded with a multi-melta, to go tank hunting.

✕ The Tornado is even more heavily armed than the standard land speeder. Able to carry a combination of anti-personnel and anti-tank weaponry, the Tornado often acts as a mobile reserve – dashing forward to exploit weaknesses in the enemy or bolstering the Space Marines' attack where they most need it.

✕ The Typhoon is a land speeder fitted with Typhoon missile launchers. Typhoon missiles are simply a larger version of the frag missiles fired by a normal missile launcher. They are excellent weapons to use against enemy infantry and light vehicles, but lack the strength to deal with more heavily armoured enemy vehicles and troops.

HEAVY SUPPORT

Devastator squads combine the flexibility of the infantryman, with the firepower of a tank. Able to take up commanding firing positions on high outcrops or in dense jungle, Devastators can bring their heavy weapons into position whatever the terrain.

The Predator tank can be configured in a number of different ways. The Annihilator optimises the Predator's tank-hunting capabilities with its multiple lascannons. Alternatively, it may be armed with heavy bolters in the sponsons to give it a powerful punch against infantry and light vehicles, while its turret-mounted tankbusting lascannon deals with any armoured foes it encounters.

The Destructor is perfectly suited to destroying swathes of enemy light vehicles and infantry with its autocannon and heavy bolters. Alternatively, when fitted with lascannons, it can prove more than a match for even the heaviest armoured vehicles in the opposing army.

The Vindicator's massive demolisher cannon is often used to breach fortified defences, allowing Terminators and Assault Squads access to enemy installations. It is also invaluable in dense terrain such as deep jungle or the twisting streets of an urban battlezone, where its comparative lack of range is unimportant.

DEVASTATOR SQUAD

	Points/Model	WS	BS	S	T	W	I	A	Ld	Sv
Space Marine	15	4	4	4	4	1	4	1	8	3+
Veteran Sergeant	+15	4	4	4	4	1	4	2	9	3+

Squad: The squad consists of a Space Marine Sergeant and between four and nine Space Marines.

Weapons: Bolters. The Sergeant may exchange his bolter for a bolt pistol and close combat weapon at no extra cost.

Options: Up to four Space Marines may have one of the following: heavy bolter at +15 pts; missile launcher at +20 pts; lascannon at +35 pts; multi-melta at +35pts; plasma cannon at +35pts.

Character: The Sergeant can be upgraded to a Veteran Sergeant with Terminator honours for +15 pts.

Transport Vehicle: The entire squad may be mounted in a Rhino at an additional cost of +50 pts or a Razorback at an additional cost of +70 pts (see Transport entry for upgrade options).

PREDATOR ANNIHILATOR

	Points	Front Armour	Side Armour	Rear Armour	BS
Annihilator	120	13	11	10	4

Type: Tank   **Crew:** Space Marines

Weapons: The Annihilator is armed with a turret-mounted twin-linked lascannon.

Options: The Annihilator may also be upgraded with two side sponsons armed with one of the following weapons: heavy bolters at +10 pts; lascannons at +25 pts.

The Annihilator may have any of the following vehicle upgrades at the cost listed in the Space Marine Armoury: dozer blades, extra armour, hunter-killer missile, pintle-mounted storm bolter, searchlight, smoke launchers. No upgrade may be chosen more than once per vehicle.

PREDATOR DESTRUCTOR

	Points	Front Armour	Side Armour	Rear Armour	BS
Destructor	100	13	11	10	4

Type: Tank   **Crew:** Space Marines

Weapons: The Destructor is armed with a turret-mounted autocannon.

Options: The Destructor can also be upgraded with two side sponsons armed with one of the following weapons: heavy bolters at +10 pts; lascannons at +25 pts.

The Destructor can have any of the following vehicle upgrades at the cost listed in the Space Marine Armoury: dozer blades, extra armour, hunter-killer missile, pintle-mounted storm bolter, searchlight, smoke launchers. No upgrade may be chosen more than once per vehicle.

VINDICATOR

	Points	Front Armour	Side Armour	Rear Armour	BS
Vindicator	120	13	11	10	4

Type: Tank   **Crew:** Space Marines

Weapons: The Vindicator is armed with a hull-mounted demolisher cannon and a storm bolter. See the Ordnance section of Warhammer 40,000 for more details.

Options: The Vindicator may have any of the following vehicle upgrades at the cost listed in the Space Marine Armoury: dozer blades, extra armour, hunter-killer missile, pintle-mounted storm bolter, searchlight, smoke launchers. No upgrade can be chosen more than once per vehicle.

LAND RAIDER

	Points	Front Armour	Side Armour	Rear Armour	BS
Land Raider	250	14	14	14	4

Type: Tank   **Crew:** Space Marines

Weapons: The Land Raider is armed with a twin-linked lascannon in each side sponson and forward firing twin-linked heavy bolters mounted on the hull.

Options: The Land Raider may be equipped with any of the following vehicle upgrades at the cost listed in the Space Marine Armoury: dozer blades, extra armour, hunter-killer missile, pintle-mounted storm bolter, searchlight, smoke launchers. No upgrade may be chosen more than once per vehicle.

Transport: The Land Raider may carry up to ten Space Marines or five Space Marine Terminators.

WHIRLWIND

	Points	Front Armour	Side Armour	Rear Armour	BS
Whirlwind	75	11	11	10	4

Type: Tank   **Crew:** Space Marines

Weapons: The Whirlwind is armed with a turret-mounted multiple missile launcher (see the Whirlwind entry in the Ordnance section of the Warhammer 40,000 rulebook).

Options: The Whirlwind may have any of the following vehicle upgrades at the cost listed in the Space Marine Armoury: dozer blades, extra armour, hunter-killer missile, pintle-mounted storm bolter, searchlight, smoke launchers. No upgrade may be chosen more than once per vehicle.

The Land Raider is one of the most potent machines of destruction in the Imperium.

The Whirlwind fires barrage after barrage of rockets into the enemy army, softening them up while the Space Marines get into position. Able to launch its attacks even when out of sight, behind a hill or jungle, often the only evidence of a Whirlwind's presence is its first payload of death roaring down from the skies.

SPACE MARINE SUMMARY

	WS	BS	S	T	W	I	A	Ld	Sv
Force Commander	5	5	4	4	3	5	3	10	3+
Commander	5	5	4	4	2	5	3	9	3+
Leader	4	4	4	4	1	4	2	9	3+
Librarian	5	5	4	4	2	5	3	9	3+
Chaplain	5	5	4	4	2	5	3	9	3+
Space Marine	4	4	4	4	1	4	1	8	3+
Vet. S/Marine	4	4	4	4	1	4	1	9	3+
Vet. Sergeant	4	4	4	4	1	4	2	9	3+
Terminator	4	4	4	4	1	4	2	9	2+
Scout	4	4	4	4	1	4	1	8	4+
S/Marine Biker	4	4	4	4(5)	1	4	1	8	3+
Scout Biker	4	4	4	4(5)	1	4	1	8	4+
Attack Bike	4	4	4	4(5)	1	4	2	8	2+

	Armour			
	Front	Side	Rear	BS
Rhino	11	11	10	4
Razorback	11	11	10	4
Land speeder	10	10	10	4
Whirlwind	11	11	10	4
Predator	13	11	10	4
Vindicator	13	11	10	4
Land Raider	14	14	14	4

				Armour				
	WS	BS	S	Front	Side	Rear	I	A
Dreadnought	4	4	6(10)	12	12	10	4	2

RANGED WEAPONS

Weapon	Range	Str.	AP	Type
Bolt pistol	12"	4	5	Pistol
Boltgun	24"	4	5	Rapid fire
Storm bolter	24"	4	5	Assault 2
Heavy bolter	36"	5	4	Heavy 3
Shotgun	12"	3	–	Assault 2
Assault cannon	24"	6	4	Heavy 3*
Autocannon	48"	7	4	Heavy 2
Lascannon	48"	9	2	Heavy 1
Flamer	Template	4	5	Assault 1
Heavy flamer	Template	5	4	Assault 1
Meltagun	12"	8	1	Assault 1*
Multi-melta	24"	8	1	Heavy 1*
Sniper rifle	36"	X	6	Heavy 1*
M. Launcher (Krak)	48"	8	3	Heavy 1*
M. Launcher (Frag)	48"	4	6	Heavy 1 Blast*
Plasma pistol	12"	7	2	Pistol*
Plasma gun	24"	7	2	Rapid fire*
Plasma cannon	36"	7	2	Heavy 1 Blast*
Typhoon Missile	48"	5	5	Heavy 1 Blast

* These weapons have additional special rules, see the Weapons section of the Warhammer 40,000 rulebook for more details.

ORDNANCE

Weapon	Range	Str.	Pene.	Type
Demolisher	24"	10	2	Ord. 1/Blast
Whirlwind	Guess 48"	5	4	Ord. 1/Blast

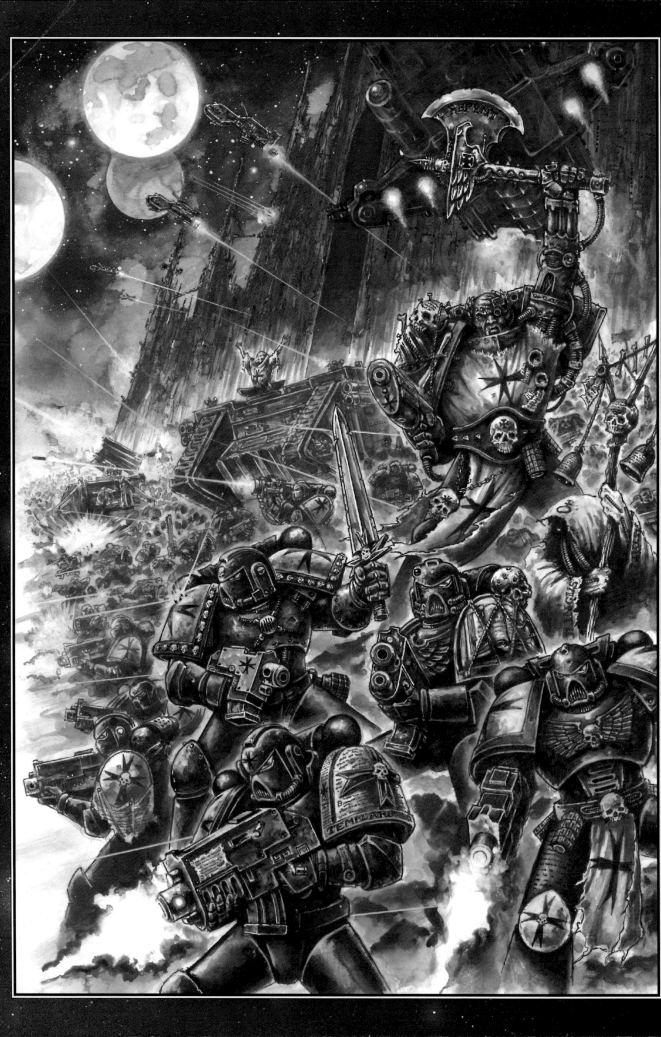

CHOOSING A SPACE MARINE ARMY

Part of the interest in collecting a Space Marine army is in building it up from a small, limited force to a large adaptable army that allows you to field exactly the right troops to succeed in any mission.

WHERE TO BEGIN?

Space Marines are one of the most versatile armies in the Warhammer 40,000 game. Not only are their basic troops very good, but they also have access to a wide variety of specialist Fast Attack, Elites and Heavy Support units.

Choosing which of these to collect can seem daunting at first, and this section of the Codex aims to give you some guidance on how to assemble a Space Marine force ready for battle.

When you are collecting your army, you must bear in mind the force organisation charts. It is these that dictate which, and how many, units you have for a battle. The best place to start is the Standard Missions force organisation chart. This is the most flexible of all the different force organisations, and if you collect an army that can be fielded within its limits, you will have a force that you should be able to field in any scenario.

As you can see from the Standard Missions force organisation chart above, you *must* have at least 1 HQ and 2 Troops units in your army. A good place to start is by buying and painting an HQ unit and two units of Troops. These two

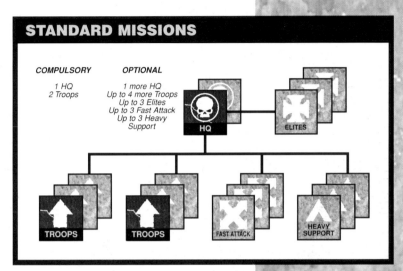

STANDARD MISSIONS

COMPULSORY
1 HQ
2 Troops

OPTIONAL
1 more HQ
Up to 4 more Troops
Up to 3 Elites
Up to 3 Fast Attack
Up to 3 Heavy Support

HQ
ELITES
TROOPS
TROOPS
FAST ATTACK
HEAVY SUPPORT

choices already allow you to fight a Standard Mission, albeit a small one. Now you can start choosing what units you'll want to expand your army with. A larger army not only means you'll be able to fight bigger battles, but it will also give you some flexibility as a commander to choose units you think will perform best in the scenario you're playing. It's also very satisfying to see your opponent's face when you reveal that new unit you've just painted – the one he hadn't planned for!

Once you have your HQ and two Troops units ready, you can start thinking about expanding your army to include more units.

The best way to find out what your army might be lacking is to play with your existing troops, and then ask yourself at the end of the battle what units you wish you'd had during the game.

It is also a good idea to talk to veteran Space Marine players, and learn from their experience and wisdom. You might also pick up some ideas of what tactics to use with different combinations of units.

Over the page you will find a guide to the different Space Marine unit types, with notes on their relative strengths and weaknesses in battle.

A basic Space Marine force made up of two Tactical squads (Troops) and a Command squad (HQ)

HQ

STRENGTHS: Heroes are powerful in close combat and good leaders. Librarians can use the powerful 'Smite' and 'Storm of Destruction' psychic powers, and Chaplains have an invulnerable save and wield power weapons.

WEAKNESSES: They all ideally need a supporting squad and have a high points cost.

HERO

LIBRARIAN

CHAPLAIN

✠ ELITES ✠

DREADNOUGHT

STRENGTHS: Big guns, awesome close combat capability, well armoured.

WEAKNESSES: Vulnerable to anti-tank weapons, highly visible target

TERMINATOR SQUAD

STRENGTHS: Superior armour save, excellent firepower and close combat ability, deep strike capability.

WEAKNESSES: Limited numbers, very high points cost!

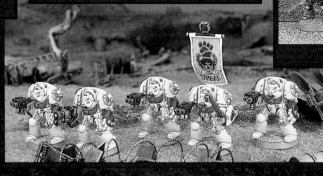

VETERAN SQUAD

STRENGTHS: Superior close combat ability, good leadership.

WEAKNESSES: Limited numbers.

↑ TROOPS ↑

TACTICAL SQUAD

STRENGTHS: Versatile, well armed and armoured.

WEAKNESSES: Not optimised for specific combat roles.

SCOUT SQUAD

STRENGTHS: Infiltrate capability, quickest troop type through difficult terrain, low points cost.

WEAKNESSES: Lightly armed and armoured.

TRANSPORT

RHINO

STRENGTHS: Carries ten Space Marines, low points cost.

WEAKNESSES: Weak armour, light weaponry.

RAZORBACK

STRENGTHS: Can pick from a good range of heavy weapons.

WEAKNESSES: Weak armour, only carries six Space Marines.

✖ FAST ATTACK ✖

LAND SPEEDER

STRENGTHS: Fast, skimmer, can be upgraded to a Tornado mounting heavy weapons.

WEAKNESSES: Weak armour, vulnerable to enemy shooting.

BIKE SQUADRON

STRENGTHS: Fast, twin-linked bolters allow you to re-roll misses.
WEAKNESSES: Fairly high points cost, limited mobility in dense terrain.

ASSAULT SQUAD

STRENGTHS: Jump packs, excellent in close combat.

WEAKNESSES: High points cost, only equipped with bolt pistols, making for weak ranged attacks.

ATTACK BIKES

STRENGTHS: Fast, mounts either a heavy bolter or multi-melta.

WEAKNESSES: Suffer from the same weaknesses as Bikes.

⋀ HEAVY SUPPORT ⋀

WHIRLWIND

PREDATOR

DEVASTATOR SQUAD

STRENGTHS
Predators: Well armed, good armour.
Whirlwinds: Fire over terrain, ordnance barrage.
Devastator Squads: Multiple heavy weapons.

WEAKNESSES
All: Must remain stationary to fire at full effect, vulnerable to assault.

EXPANDING YOUR ARMY

So you've got some Troops and an HQ, but what's next? Here are a couple of different ways you can expand your force into a sizeable army.

Once you have two Troops units and an HQ, you can look at expanding your army with more units. A good way to start is to collect a unit from each of the other categories in the army list – Elites, Fast Attack and Heavy Support.

You can see this in Alan's army below. He has expanded his force to include a squad of Terminators, a Land Speeder Tornado and a Whirlwind. He has also added a Librarian as a second HQ choice. Now he has at least one unit from each army list category.

Experienced Warhammer 40,000 players often have an idea of how their army will turn out before they start collecting. They pick their army with a theme in mind, concentrating on units which suit their style of play or they find most appealing.

Paul's army below is a good example of this. His force focuses on rapid attack, and he's expanded it to include three choices from the Fast Attack category. To complement this emphasis on speed, Paul's also given his Tactical squad a Rhino, so they can quickly get stuck in.

DARK CRUSADERS FORCE

Alan Merrett

HQ (Commander & Librarian)

ELITES (Terminator Squad)

HEAVY SUPPORT (Whirlwind)

TROOPS (Tactical Squad)

TROOPS (Tactical Squad)

FAST ATTACK (Land Speeder Tornado)

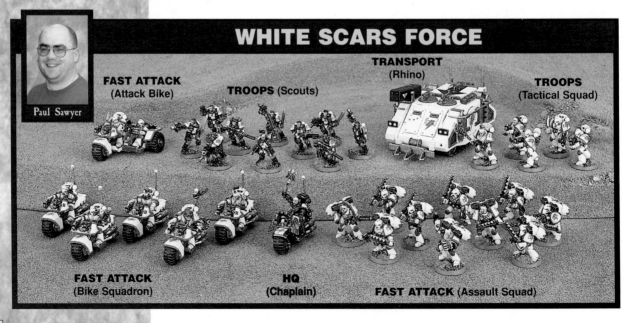

WHITE SCARS FORCE

Paul Sawyer

FAST ATTACK (Attack Bike)

TROOPS (Scouts)

TRANSPORT (Rhino)

TROOPS (Tactical Squad)

FAST ATTACK (Bike Squadron)

HQ (Chaplain)

FAST ATTACK (Assault Squad)

SPACE MARINE TACTICS

On this page are three different battle plans for a Space Marine army. These are just the basic ideas, and leave plenty of room for you to tailor these tactics to your own forces and different opponents.

Predator gives supporting fire. Tactical squad can support or advance as necessary.

Command squad and Terminators advance into enemy.

Bike squad advances quickly up edge of table, whilst Scouts push forward through jungle.

ALL-OUT ATTACK

• Use to capture ground.

• Gets Space Marines into firefights and close combat, where they excel.

• Good against enemies with lots of Heavy Support and few specialist assault troops, such as tank-heavy Imperial Guard.

Bike squad moves to where enemy attack is strongest.

Tactical squad gives covering fire.

Terminators hold or counter-attack as necessary.

Command squad advances into cover of ruins.

Predator gives supporting fire. Scouts protect Predator against assault, and counter-attack enemy moving through jungle.

SOLID DEFENCE

• Use to hold ground.

• Good against armies with specialist assault troops, like Tyranids and Chaos.

• Good against fast enemies who may surround your smaller force, like Eldar.

Bike squad, Command squad and Terminators attack along edge of table.

Predator and Tactical squad give supporting fire.

Scouts in ruins, ready to attack when enemy is weakened.

REFUSED FLANK

• Use against armies that field vastly superior numbers, like Orks and Imperial Guard.

• Prevents enemy bringing numbers to bear – enemy spread across whole battlefield, so units on opposite flank out of range of Space Marines.

• Attack one part of enemy army at a time and destroy it totally before attacking next section of enemy army.

• Allows Space Marines to capture ground.

SPACE MARINE CHAPTER COLOURS

There are reputed to be a thousand Space Marine Chapters, each with its own unique uniform and heraldry. Here are just a few of their colour schemes, which you can use as they are, or to serve as inspiration for a Chapter you've invented.

Above each picture we've shown the Chapter badge and a colour swatch that tells you what basic colour was used to paint the model. Each picture also has either a white or black dot next to it, indicating what colour was used as an undercoat.

SKULL WHITE	CHAOS BLACK	GOLDEN YELLOW	CAMO GREEN
WHITE SCARS	RAVEN GUARD	MARAUDERS	RAPTORS

BLOOD RED	ULTRAMARINES BLUE	SKULL WHITE	SNOT GREEN
RAMPAGERS	ULTRAMARINES	WHITE CONSULS	AURORA CHAPTER

CODEX GREY	CHAOS BLACK	SCORPION GREEN	MITHRIL SILVER
REVILERS	BLACK TEMPLARS	SONS OF MEDUSA	DOOM EAGLES

SPACE MARINE MARKINGS

SQUAD BADGES

TACTICAL SQUAD

ASSAULT SQUAD

DEVASTATOR SQUAD

VETERAN SQUAD

COMMAND SQUAD

NUMBERS

CHAPTER BADGE

Space Marine Chapters use many different methods to distinguish between the squads within a Company. Many use different badges to mark the squad type, eg Tactical, Assault, etc. Other Chapters simply number the squads in a Company. Some Chapters do both and combine a tactical badge with a squad number. Sometimes a Chapter's different Companies are distinguished by a Company colour. This may be used as a trim colour on shoulder pads or some other part of the armour.

ARMY BADGES

Space Marine Commanders often assign army badges to their forces to identify the troops under their command during a war.

 MIDNIGHT BLUE

 GOLDEN YELLOW

 CHAOS BLACK

 BLOOD RED

CRIMSON FISTS

IMPERIAL FISTS

IRON HANDS

RED TALONS

 BOLT GUN METAL

 CHAOS BLACK

 REGAL BLUE & SKULL WHITE

 GOLDEN YELLOW & BLOOD RED

SILVER SKULLS

SCYTHES OF THE EMPEROR

EAGLE WARRIORS

HOWLING GRIFFONS

HOW TO PAINT AN ULTRAMARINE

Choosing your force is just the first part of collecting an army. Once you have an idea what you want, you need to get some miniatures painted! This may seem a daunting prospect, but if you follow the advice on these pages, you'll hopefully find it's easier than it appears.

As you will have seen on the previous pages, a Space Marine army consists of ten or more miniatures, and may have up to sixty plus! Many gamers find it is best to paint miniatures in batches of five to ten models, rather than painting them individually.

Painting in batches has a number of benefits. Firstly, you can get into a steady routine so that you don't start from scratch for each model. Secondly, by the time you've painted a colour on the last model, the first model should be ready for the next colour, so you're not sitting around watching paint dry!

It is also important to remember that you're painting an army to play games with – each model doesn't have to be a masterpiece! On the tabletop, the overall impression of a unit will count for more than any amount of individual highlighting and attention to detail. Remember this when you're painting and you'll find that painting a whole army doesn't take as long as you might think.

If you follow the steps below, you should be able to paint a perfectly acceptable Space Marine unit without too much difficulty and within a reasonable amount of time.

❶ After cleaning up your Space Marine models and assembling them, the first thing to do is give them an undercoat. The best way of undercoating models is to use white aerosol spray. Spray undercoating is a real time-saver, as you can spray a whole batch of models in one go, rather than having to paint each one individually with a brush. Once the models are undercoated, set them aside for a while to dry before moving on to the next stage.

❷ Now you're ready to paint the first coat of colour onto your Ultramarines. Using Ultramarines Blue paint and a fine detail brush, carefully apply the paint to all areas of the Space Marines except the chest eagle, gun and shoulder pad trims. Don't worry if you make a few mistakes and accidentally paint over some of the bits that won't be blue. You can always paint over any mistakes you make at a later stage.

❸ By the time you've painted the last of your models blue, the first ones you did will probably be dry. Now you can apply other colours to your Space Marines. Paint their shoulder pad trims and chest eagles yellow, and use red paint for the casings of the bolt guns. Any areas left white after that should be painted black. Try painting a single colour on all of your models first, before moving onto the next colour. You'll find you finish them a lot quicker this way.

❹ Now it's time for the last few finishing touches. Carefully paint the eyes of each Space Marine red. Next, using silver paint, paint over the remaining black areas of each model (the gun and bits of the helmet). Finally, paint the bases of the models a colour which matches the colour of your gaming surface (we've used green in our example).

Your Ultramarines are now finished and ready for battle!

Although we've used an Ultramarine in our stage-by-stage example above, the same basic principles apply to painting Space Marines from any Chapter. Looking at pages 22-23, if for instance you decided you wanted to paint some White Consuls, you'd simply substitute blue paint for white when following the steps above.

A finished Tactical squad of Ultramarines. Using the method described above, this squad was painted in under an hour.

PAINTING SPACE MARINES

These two pages detail a variety of different painting techniques which you can use to paint your Space Marines. Each can be used to achieve a particular effect, and with a bit of practice you'll settle on a style of painting that suits your needs in terms of quality balanced against speed.

Most of the techniques discussed below can be combined together, and as you will see, some work better with certain colours or on certain parts of the model. Like any skill, learning how to paint miniatures takes time and practice. Don't be afraid to experiment. Remember, painting is meant to be part of the fun of collecting an army, not a chore!

LOOKING AFTER YOUR PAINTS & BRUSHES

A workman is only as good as his tools, and if you try painting with a brush with bristles pointing in all directions, you'll end up with stray flecks of colour everywhere! To keep a good point on your brushes, always store them upright in a jar. When painting, use an old brush to transfer paint from the pot to a palette (a kitchen tile is excellent for this) so that you're not dunking the brush up to the handle into the pot. Also make sure you wash the brush regularly while painting to stop paint drying in the bristles.

Citadel paintbrushes come in a variety of different sizes, from a fine detail brush up to a large drybrush. Most of your painting can probably be done with a standard brush and a detail brush, although you may find a basecoat brush better for painting broad areas such as shoulder pads and greaves. A fine detail brush can be used once you've had some practice and want to try painting things like eyes and other tiny details! The special drybrushes are made of stiffer fibres, and when painting bolters and other metal areas you'll find they won't wear out as quickly.

UNDERCOATING

Aerosol sprays are great for undercoating your miniatures – they're fast and give a smooth finish. When using sprays always work in a well ventilated area, preferably outside, to stop fumes building up.

A black undercoat is best for dark colour schemes such as black, dark blue, or dark green. Use white for lighter colour schemes, like yellow, red or light blue.

PAINTING METAL

To paint a metal area such as a bolter, first paint it black. Get some silver paint on your brush and then wipe most of it off on a tissue so that only a residue is left. Lightly brush back and forth over the black and the colour will be picked up on the raised parts. More or less coats will change how bright the metal ends up.

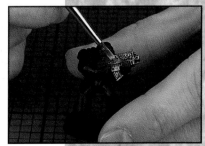

USING INKS

Inks are mostly used to provide a darker colour – adding shading to your miniatures. As inks are thin, they will settle in the recesses and flow off raised areas, creating instant areas of shadow when painted onto a model. Using inks in this way is sometimes referred to as an ink wash.

As you can see in the photographs above, inks can be used on faces (use Flesh ink), chest eagles (use an appropriate darker colour) and metallic areas (use Black ink, or Black ink mixed with a little bit of Blue ink).

If you have a steady hand, you can also use inks to paint a thin line into areas where armour plates join, hands meet weapons etc. This helps define different parts of the model and can be used to make certain features stand out.

You can also use inks on flat areas of armour to make a deeper, richer colour. The method for this is the same – paint over the entire area with ink and allow it to dry.

It is important to give inks plenty of time to dry, as they take longer than paint. If you put the next colour on too soon, it will mix with the ink and run everywhere.

BASING WITH FLOCK

You can finish off a base quickly and simply with modelling flock. Paint the base green and allow the paint to dry. Then paint on a layer of PVA glue thinned down with some water. While the glue is still wet, dip the base into a pot of flock and then shake off any excess.

BASING WITH SAND

You can also base miniatures with sand. Paint the base with thinned down PVA glue and then dip it into some sand. Once dry, paint the sand a colour that matches your tabletop battlefield. Some people even brush over the sand with a lighter colour for a highlighted effect.

TRANSFERS

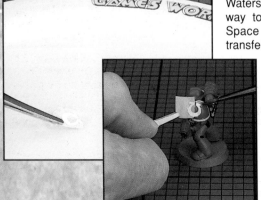

Waterslide transfers are a simple way to apply markings to your Space Marines. Cut out a transfer and leave it in a saucer of water for about 30 seconds. Then, using a pair of tweezers and a brush, slide the transfer off its backing paper and onto your model. Use the corner of a tissue to dab away any excess water from the model.

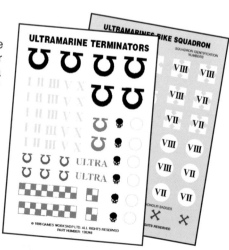

MAKING TERRAIN

A nicely painted army fighting over a well-modelled battlefield looks superb, and you should give some time and thought to building up a collection of battlefield terrain. The easiest way is to simply buy what you need. However, many gamers find they enjoy making their own terrain, specifically tailored to their needs.

Games Workshop's *How to Make Wargames Terrain* is packed with loads of information on making terrain — everything from basic, easy-to-make scenery, through to more challenging projects.

Games Workshop produces a wide range of card and plastic terrain kits that are ideal for any Warhammer 40,000 battlefield.

This page gives a couple of ideas for modelling projects. Terrain pieces such as a gun emplacement or Imperial outpost are quite challenging to make, but they're both good examples of how you can create spectacular terrain using very ordinary materials. You should keep a constant look out for odds and ends that can be turned into great looking scenery. Cardboard tubes and boxes, packing materials, old paint pots, camera film cases, yogurt pots, polystyrene, bits of chain and wire and all sorts of other stuff can all be turned into dramatic battlefield features for your Space Marines to fight over.

GUN EMPLACEMENT

M DF board or thick cardboard should be used to make the base of this model. The main structure (the area sprayed black) is made from bits of card glued together. Once the structure is dry, place it on a block of styrofoam and draw around it. Cut this outline out of the styrofoam, leaving a hole for the structure to slot into, then glue the styrofoam to the base and cut away any overhanging parts. You can also cut into it to give it a sloping, contoured edge. Slot the main structure into the styrofoam and glue it down.

Next, glue a layer of wire mesh to the floor of the structure, then place a layer of card over the top with holes cut in it for the mesh to show through. Coat the base and the styrofoam slopes with textured paint (ie, paint with sand mixed into it) and stick some gravel to the model with PVA glue to give added texture. Once all these stages are complete, the gun emplacement is ready to paint.

IMPERIAL OUTPOST

T he basic structure of the outpost is made using the same materials as the gun emplacement. Once complete, extra details can be added, such as the plastic jungle trees and the watchtower on top of the outpost. Paint the trees and the outpost separately, before you glue the two together, as you'll find it difficult to paint the trees once they've been stuck on.

The watchtower is made from spare bits of plastic taken from a model train set, but could have just as easily been made from strips of card. Cover the styrofoam hill and the structure in textured paint and flock the base after you've painted it, but before you glue the trees on.

Ultramarines Rhino, Razorback & Predator

Crimson Fists Predator & Dreadnought

Black Templars Razorback

Imperial Fists Predator & Bike Squadron

"To admit defeat is
to blaspheme against
the Emperor"

Roboute Guilliman –
Primarch of the Ultramarines

Silver Skulls Razorback

Ultramarines Predator

On these pages you can see a selection of Space Marine vehicles painted by Games Workshop's 'Eavy Metal team. You can use them as guides for your own vehicle colour schemes, and advice for painting vehicles can be found on the following pages.

Ultramarines Bike Squadron & Attack Bike

Crimson Fists Dreadnought

Storm Lords Rhino

Ultramarines Whirlwind

HOW TO PAINT SPACE MARINE VEHICLES

Space Marine vehicles can be painted very quickly, however big or complicated they may look. The steps below use a Predator tank as an example, but there is no reason why the same process cannot be applied to any kind of Space Marine vehicle – from bikes to land speeders.

❶

First you need to prime your model with an undercoat. White aerosol spray paint is great for applying as an undercoat. Spray the model in a well ventilated area (preferably outdoors), and then leave it to dry.

❷

The next stage is to apply the first coat of colour to the model. Decide what basic colour your vehicle is going to be, then paint the entire model in that colour. Better still, if you can find spray paint in your chosen colour then you can just spray the colour all over your model.

❸

Identify the parts of the model you want to look metallic once it's finished, and paint them black. This is because metal paints works best when painted on black.

❹

To add highlights to your model, use a lighter shade of the basic colour. Add some paint to your brush and then wipe most of the paint off on some tissue. Now gently stroke the brush over any sharp edges on your model.

❺

At this point, you can paint all the areas you painted black earlier with a metal colour. We've used Boltgun Metal for our Predator. Sometimes metal can look a bit too 'clean', in which case you can add some contrast by applying a watered-down coat of black ink over the metal.

❻

Areas that were left plain black after stage 5 have been highlighted with light grey. Finally, apply waterslide transfers to the model to represent its Chapter badge and other markings. The vehicle is now ready to play games with!

The finished Predator and a Space Marine squad ready for gaming.

ADDING EXTRA DETAIL TO VEHICLES

SILVER SKULLS RAZORBACK

One really easy way of making your vehicles look battle-scarred is to use a modelling knife and cut lots of small chips and scratches in the surface of the plastic to simulate bullet holes, dents and other forms of battle damage.

This Space Marine bike has been personalised by simply gluing a chainsword on to the side of it.

IMPERIAL FISTS PREDATOR ANNIHILATOR

IMPERIAL FISTS SPACE MARINE BIKE

Paper flags, hand painted and then glued on.

The fuel canister glued to the front of the Rhino was taken from a Warhammer 40,000 Battlefield Accessories sprue.

This aerial is made from a length of thin wire.

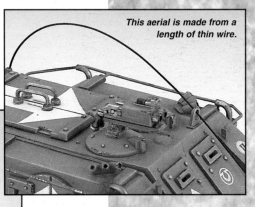

ULTRAMARINES RHINO

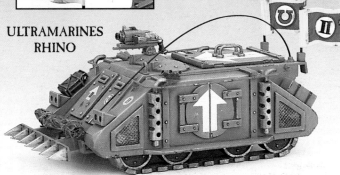

This tarpaulin is a rolled up strip of tissue paper tied off at each end with thread, then painted with PVA glue to make it solid.

'EAVY METAL
SHOWCASE

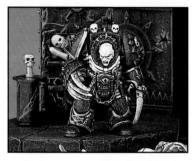

Many hobbyists find that painting Citadel miniatures is a rewarding and satisfying activity in its own right. On this page are a few examples of some superbly painted Space Marines. Whilst it would not be practical to attempt to paint an entire army in this fashion, models like these can form an impressive centrepiece for an army or, more likely, a dramatic and colourful display to decorate your games room! Some hobbyists even enter their models into the Golden Demon painting competition, held every year at Games Day.

▲ *This amazing diorama is by Games Workshop miniature designer Mike McVey. It features the epic scene where the Emperor and Warmaster Horus finally clash in single combat.*

◀*Far Left: Space Marine Scout incorporating a green and brown camouflage scheme, painted by Martin Footitt. Left: Imperial Fists Space Marine Scout painted by Ben Jefferson.*

▼*Ultramarines Veteran Sergeant, painted by Martin Footitt.*

▲ *From left to right: Ultramarines Standard Bearer painted by Richard Baker; Marneus Calgar painted by Neil Hodgson; Tigurius painted by Paul Muller.*

APPENDIX

From here on in the rest of the Codex is given over to the Appendix section. The Appendix includes all kinds of information which does not fit into the army list itself. This includes rules for wargear and vehicle upgrades noted in the Space Marine Armoury section, details of a selection of named Space Marine characters and a special Space Marine scenario.

Also, we have compiled a series of reports and commentaries which shed extra light onto the arcane history and organisation of the Space Marine Chapters. We hope that these provide an interesting read as well as being of some assistance to players creating their own Space Marine Chapters or who are running campaigns.

Captain Karrack spoke the Litany of Sealing as the Thunderhawk gunship's front ramp swung down with a clang. He felt his helmet lock down onto its neck ring as the atmosphere inside the gunship puffed out into a cloud of ice crystals, hungrily sucked out by the freezing void. The Ultramarines deployed in Ferrus formation as planned, thirty armoured figures debouching onto the grey, dusty surface in under six seconds. The Gunship's engines screamed back to life and with a blast of heat and dust it was gone, angling up and back to join the cold stars of the firmament above.

Grey rocks and craters stretched toward the horizon, which looked less than a league away thanks to the moon's size. Karrack took a bearing and gestured, the Space Marines set off, splitting into six squads as they went and spreading out to encircle a vast crater ahead. They halted at the rim and scanned the Imperial research station below. No signs of violence, no shot-scarred walls or breached domes, even the lights still burned. Karrack took Squad Veritas and moved forward to investigate.

They were half way across the crater floor when the traitors opened fire. Laser bolts ripped from the shadows, burning at their armour and scorching the rocks. An instant later the Space Marines on overwatch around the crater rim pumped bolter shells into their assailants with machine-like precision. Karrack saw bodies leap and contort as the mass-reactive rounds blew them apart, their blood billowing out in clouds of scarlet frost.

Karrack led Squad Veritas in a charge towards the main entry lock. Great-coated Guardsmen stood forth to bar his way, eyes wild above their respirators as they clumsily swung their lasguns to bear. Karrack's bolter blew a hole straight through the one on the right and a backhand blow crushed the skull of the other. The clouds of frozen blood and slight weightlessness made him feel as if he were fighting underwater. He punched the lock entry code and readied a frag grenade while it cycled. Sure enough as the inner door opened a storm of laser bolts scoured the lock. The exploding frag grenade made the traitors duck back and by the time they recovered Karrack and the other Space Marines were upon them.

Once the fighting was over they searched the base from one end to the other but found no other survivors. Some of the Adepts had taken their own lives but others had been killed by their own guards, and many were missing altogether. In the central chamber they found the borehole down to whatever had been discovered under the ice. Whatever had been there, was now gone.

SPACE MARINE WARGEAR

The following rules describe how all of the specialised equipment used by Space Marines works during a battle. These rules tend to be more detailed than those included in the Warhammer 40,000 rulebook, and they supersede them if they are different. Any items not listed here function exactly as described in the Warhammer 40,000 rulebook.

Artificer Armour: Artificer armour is built by master craftsmen and offers even greater protection than a normal suit of Space Marine power armour. It may be taken as an upgrade for a model wearing power armour and increases the armour's save to 2+. Note that, although this armour gives the same protection as Terminator armour, items that are 'Terminators only' cannot be used with it.

Auspex: An auspex is a short-ranged scanner used by Space Marines to detect hidden enemy troops. If enemy infiltrators set up within 4D6" of a model with an auspex, then that model is allowed to take a 'free' shot at them (or sound the alarm in a Raid scenario). If the model is part of a unit then the whole unit may shoot. These shots are taken before the battle begins, and may cause the infiltrators to fall back. The normal shooting rules apply.

Bionics: Bionics allow a Space Marine who has suffered a crippling injury to return to service, but are unlikely to improve or enhance his abilities. However there is a chance an attack or shot will hit a bionic part causing less damage, eg a shot that would cripple a leg will only cause mild damage to a bionic leg. To represent this, if a model with bionics is killed, instead of removing it, place the model on its side. Roll a D6 at the start of the next turn: on a roll of a 6 the model is stood back up with 1 wound, but on any other roll it is removed as a casualty.

Chainfist: A chainfist is simply a power fist fitted with an attachment designed to carve through armoured bulkheads or armoured vehicles. It is treated exactly as a power fist, but roll 2D6 for its armour penetration value.

Chapter Banner: Chapter banners combine the effect of a holy relic and a sacred standard (see their entries for details).

Combi-weapons: These are basically two weapons joined together, giving the Space Marine a choice of two weapons to fire instead of one. A Space Marine who is armed with a combi-weapon may choose which of the weapons he is going to use in the shooting phase. The bolter may be fired any number of times, but the other weapon may only be fired once per battle. Note that you may not choose to fire both weapons at once.

Crozius Arcanum: The crozius arcanum is both a Space Marine Chaplain's badge of office and a weapon. In game terms it is treated as a power weapon.

Cyclone Missile Launcher: The Cyclone is a specially designed missile launcher that can be used by Space Marines in Terminator armour. The weapon in the Terminator's left hand is replaced with a special targeting device which allows him to fire the Cyclone and his storm bolter in the same shooting phase. The Cyclone otherwise counts as a missile launcher with frag and krak missiles.

Force Weapon: Force weapons are potent psychic weapons that can only be used by a trained psyker such as a Librarian. They are treated as a power weapon, but can unleash a psychic attack that can kill an opponent outright. Roll to hit, to wound and to save as normal. Then, as long as at least one wound has been inflicted, make a Psychic test for the psyker against one opponent wounded by the weapon. The normal rules for using psychic powers apply, and you can not use another psychic ability in the same turn. If the test is passed then the opponent is slain outright, no matter how many wounds it has (but count the actual amount inflicted for determining which side won the assault).

Note that a force weapon has no special effect against targets that don't have wounds, eg Dreadnoughts, vehicles, etc. Also note that you only take one Psychic test no matter how many wounds were inflicted.

Holy Relic: A model bearing a holy relic may reveal it once per battle. This may be done at any time, as long as the model with the relic does not move during the same turn it is revealed. On the turn the relic is revealed all Space Marines within 2D6" get a +1 Attack bonus for the rest of that turn. Note that the relic may be revealed in an opposing player's turn if you wish.

Iron Halo: The Iron Halo is a special reward given to Space Marines who show exceptional initiative or bravery in battle. In game terms it has the same effect as a rosarius, giving the model a 4+ invulnerable save that may be used instead of the model's normal armour save. No more than one model per army may have an Iron Halo and any model wearing Terminator armour or who has a rosarius may not be given this piece of wargear.

Jump Packs: Jump packs allow models to move 12" per turn in the movement phase, and ignore difficult terrain as they move. Characters leading a Command squad or who are part of a unit can only use a jump pack if all models in the unit have jump packs.

Space Marine models who are wearing jump packs can be dropped from low-flying Thunderhawk gunships, using their jump packs to swoop down on to the battlefield. To represent this tactic they can set up using the *Deep Strike* rules, but only if the mission allows for Deep Strike to be used. If the mission does not allow troops to use Deep Strike then the model must set up normally with the rest of the army.

Lightning Claws: Lightning claws count as a power weapon and the model wearing them may re-roll any to wound rolls that fail to wound. Models who are armed with Lightning claws only receive the +1 Attack modifier for an additional close combat weapon if the second weapon is also another Lightning claw, as they are generally used as a pair.

Master-Crafted Weapons: A master-crafted weapon follows the normal rules for the weapon, except that you may re-roll one failed to hit roll per turn. Master-crafted weapons are taken as an upgrade for a weapon that is already being carried by a model and should be represented by a suitably ornate weapon on the model itself. Please note that you may *not* master-craft grenades!

The cost listed in the Wargear section is in addition to the cost of the weapon itself (eg a master-crafted power weapon costs 15+15=30 pts). However, only the upgrade costs are taken against the 100 points limit on wargear for a model (so the master-crafted power weapon above would count as 15 points against the 100 points limit, not 30 points).

Narthecium: Narthecium is the name given to the medi-packs used by Space Marine Apothecaries. They allow you to ignore the first failed saving throw each turn for the unit that the Apothecary is with. The Narthecium may not be used on any model who has been unfortunate enough to suffer 'Instant Death' (eg, hit by a weapon with twice its Toughness) or that has been hit by a weapon that allows no save. It may also not be used if the Apothecary is in base contact with an enemy model.

Psychic Hood: Psychic hoods allow a Space Marine Librarian to nullify an opposing psychic's power. Declare that you'll use the Psychic hood after an opponent has successfully made a Psychic test, but before they have used the power. Each player then rolls a D6 and adds their model's Leadership value to the score. If the Space Marine Librarian beats the opposing model's score then the psychic power is nullified and may not be used that turn. If the opposing model's score is equal or higher, it may use its psychic power as normal.

Purity Seals: If a model who is wearing purity seals falls back, roll one extra D6 for its fall back distance, and then pick the D6 results you want in order to determine the distance fallen back. If a model with purity seals is part of a unit then this ability applies to the whole unit, not just to the model with the purity seals.

Reductor: The reductor is one of the devices used by an Apothecary to retrieve the progenoid gland from fallen Space Marines. These glands are vital for ensuring the continued existence of the Chapter. To represent this, when playing a scenario that uses victory points to determine the winner, you will get 1 victory point back for each slain Space Marine at the end of the battle, but only as long as the Apothecary is still alive himself.

Rosarius: All Chaplains wear a rosarius, a small amulet bestowed upon them by the Ecclesiarchy of Terra. The rosarius generates a small energy field that provides the Chaplain with an invulnerable 4+ save. This may be taken instead of the Chaplain's normal armour save.

Sacred Standard: Add +1 to the Space Marine combat resolution score of any assault that takes place within 6" of a sacred standard. However, if the model bearing the standard is slain in close combat, then the enemy model that slew him captures the standard and gets the bonus from then on. It is possible for a standard to change hands several times in a single battle, as long as the model holding the standard is slain in close combat each time.

Servo-Arm: Many Techmarines are equipped with a powerful servo-arm that can be used to carry out hasty battlefield repairs. The servo-arm counts as a power fist in close combat. It always hits on a 4+ and is rolled separately from the Techmarine's own Attacks. In addition it may be used at the start of any Space Marine turn to repair an immobilised vehicle that is in base contact with the Techmarine. On a D6 roll of a 6 the vehicle is repaired and may move normally.

Signum: The signum is a special form of communication device that allows the Techmarine to access a myriad of useful battlefield targeting information, and then pass it on to his fellow battle brothers. In game terms it allows you, each turn, to re-roll one missed to hit shooting roll for the Command squad that the Techmarine belongs to.

Space Marine Bike: Space Marine bikes are fitted with twin-linked bolters and increase the rider's Toughness by +1 point. Space Marine characters that have a Command squad or are part of a unit may only be given a bike if all of the models in the unit are also on bikes.

Storm Shield: A storm shield is a small metal shield that has an energy field generator built into it. The energy field is too small to be of much use against ranged attacks, but is very useful in close combat. A model that has a storm shield may take a 4+ invulnerable save in close combat, instead of its normal armour save. The save may only be used against one opponent per turn (the defender chooses who to use it against), and it may not be combined with a rosarius or iron halo save.

Teleport Homer: Teleport homers produce a signal that can be locked onto by teleporting troops. If the template used by the teleporting Terminators to make a *Deep Strike* is centred on the model with the homer, then they won't scatter. Note that the homer only works for troops who are teleporting, not for troops entering play using jump packs, drop pods or other means of transport. Also note that the homer must be on the table at the start of the turn it is used.

Terminator Armour: Due to the powerful exo-skeleton and power sources built into their armour, Space Marines in Terminator armour are capable of moving and firing with heavy weapons. On the other hand, this armour is somewhat heavy and cumbersome so Space Marine Terminators are not able to pursue a more lightly armoured foe when they flee. To represent this, Terminators that win a close combat may only consolidate; they will not be able to advance.

A model wearing Terminator armour has a 2+ armour save and adds +1 to its Attacks characteristic. Also, any model wearing Terminator armour can be teleported onto the battlefield, and set up using the *Deep Strike* rules, but only if the mission allows for Deep Strike to be used. If the mission does not allow troops to use the Deep Strike rules then the model must set up normally with the rest of the army.

Terminator Honours: A model with Terminator honours adds +1 to its Attacks characteristic. Note that this bonus has already been included in the characteristics of Veteran Sergeants and any Space Marines who are equipped with Terminator armour, and therefore may not be taken again.

Thunder Hammer: Thunder hammers release a terrific blast of energy when they strike an opponent. A thunder hammer counts as a power fist, but any model wounded by it and not killed may not attack again until the end of the next assault phase. Vehicles struck by a thunder hammer are 'crew shaken', in addition to any other results they suffer.

SPACE MARINE VEHICLE UPGRADES

J ust as with choosing wargear for your Space Marine troops and characters, the upgrades you choose for your vehicle should be represented on the model itself, eg if you choose to upgrade your vehicle with searchlights, then the model of your vehicle should have searchlights on it too. Note that when choosing upgrades no vehicle can have the same upgrade more than once.

Dozer Blade: Vehicles equipped with dozer blades can re-roll a failed Difficult Terrain test as long as they are not going to be moving more than 6" that turn.

Extra Armour: Some Space Marine vehicle crews add additional armour plating to their vehicles to provide a little extra protection. Vehicles equipped with extra armour count 'crew stunned' results on the Vehicle Damage tables as a 'crew shaken' result instead.

Hunter-Killer Missile: Hunter-killer missiles are a common upgrade for Imperial vehicles. They are treated as a krak missile with unlimited range and can only be used once per battle.

Pintle-Mounted Storm bolter: Pintle-mounted storm bolters are fixed to the outside of a vehicle and can either be used by a crewman from an open hatch or by remote control from inside the vehicle. They are treated as an extra storm bolter that can be used in addition to any other weapons the vehicle has. Note that this means that a vehicle that moves can fire one weapon *and* the pintle-mounted storm bolter.

Searchlight: Searchlights are only of any use in missions where the rules for night fighting are being used. They allow one enemy unit spotted by the vehicle to be fired at by any other Space Marines that are in range and have a line of fire (the enemy unit has been illuminated by the vehicle's searchlight). However, a vehicle that uses a searchlight can be fired on by any enemy units in their next turn, as they can see the searchlight shining out into the dark.

Smoke Launchers: Some vehicles have small launchers mounted onto them that carry smoke charges (or a more sophisticated equivalent in the case of skimmers). These are used to temporarily hide the vehicle behind concealing clouds of smoke especially if the vehicle is moving out in the open. Once per game, after completing its move, a vehicle with smoke launchers can trigger them (it doesn't matter how far it moved). Place some cotton wool around the vehicle to show it is concealed. The vehicle may not fire in the same turn as it used its smoke launchers, but any penetrating hits scored by the enemy in their next shooting phase count as glancing hits. After the enemy's turn the smoke disperses with no further effect.

Perseverance and silence are the highest virtues.

MARNEUS CALGAR, MASTER OF THE ULTRAMARINES

Marneus Augustus Calgar is the renowned master of the Ultramarines, and his countless exploits while defeating the enemies of the Emperor (may his divine light always guide us!) have earned him fame throughout the Imperium. In particular his stubborn defence and ultimate crushing defeat of the Tyranids during the First Tyrannic War has become the stuff of legend amongst the more vulgar elements of the population on those planets that owe allegiance to the Ultramarines. But fame and glory ever begets jealousy and spite, and these heroic tales, fuelled by Marneus' fierce (some might say intractable) pride, have earned him and his brethren many high-ranking enemies. While I can find no direct evidence, it seems probable that these enemies engineered the now infamous Court of Inquiry into Marneus' actions during the suppression of the uprising on Colony Beta/54 where Marneus was quite rightly exonerated of all charges, (if his excellency will allow me to put forward my own, very humble, opinion). Recent reports that Marneus was slain during the defence of Ichar IV appear to be based upon nothing but base rumour and tawdry gossip, and all the reliable evidence I have found indicates he continues to lead the Ultramarines to this day.

"Leaders of the Adeptus Astartes" - A Most Secret Report, Compiled for His Most Supreme Excellency the Paternoval Envoy by his Humble Servant Master Maximus Pliny.

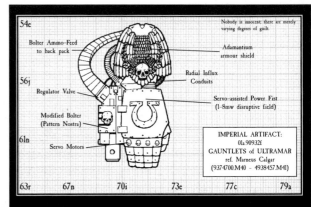

The Gauntlets of Ultramar

The Ultramarines have fought for the Emperor on many strange alien worlds, over ten thousand years of Imperial history. During that time they have discovered and explored uncounted alien worlds where long-dead civilisations have yielded great secrets. Strange and potent artefacts have been uncovered, many of which now reside within the Ultramarines' fortress on Macragge.

Amongst the oldest and most revered are the Gauntlets of Ultramar, won by the Ultramarines' Primarch in hand-to-hand combat with a fell and mighty Champion of the Dark Gods of Chaos. These weapons are of unknown origin and no Techno-Magus has ever succeeded in penetrating their armoured shell to examine the mechanism within. The Gauntlets are worn only by the Master of the Ultramarines, Lord Macragge, and at other times rest within a crystal case within the Shrine of the Great Primarch himself.

698.M41: The Corinthian Crusade - Calgar is elected leader of a combined Space Marine force including the Ultramarines, Lamenters, Marines Errant, Angels of Absolution and Silver Skulls on a seven year crusade. Under his determined leadership the Ork empire of Charadon suffered a series of heavy defeats, delaying the invasion of Waaagh Argluk by some thirty years

704.M41: Siege of Tulwa - Calgar led the infiltration force that destroyed the Fortress of Pain, established by Chaos Space Marines of the Iron Warriors Legion.

745.M41: Battle of Macragge - Calgar led the fleet of Ultramar against the Tyranid Behemoth Hivefleet. After a long and bloody struggle the Tyranids were defeated but the entire Ultramarines First company was wiped out.

759.M41: Scouring of Quintarn - Calgar took personal command of forces driving out Ork scavengers who had captured the triple system of Quintarn, Tarentus and Masali in the aftermath of Hivefleet Behemoth.

807.M41: Purgation of Jhanna - Calgar led two Ultramarine companies in the recapture of the rebellious oceanic cities of Omon and Vorlencia. Despite the rebels' Chaos Space Marine allies Calgar succeeded in recapturing both cities largely intact.

861.M41: Battle of Arconar - Calgar defeated a powerful coalition of Eldar Raiders on the feral world of Arconar, scattering their forces and capturing their bases both on and off world.

879.M41: Battle of Knarts Landing - Calgar eliminated a rebel army led by General Dornal in a thirty day battle on the industrial world of Knarts Landing. Ultramarine casualties in the engagement were less than 17%.

944.M41: Balur Crusade - Calgar was elected leader of a crusading Space Marine force operating against worlds along the Eastern fringe. Operations began with the scouring of Ork-held Balur and ended with the devastation of Boros.

995.M41: Defence of Ichar IV - Calgar acted as supreme commander in the defence of Ichar IV, a vital industrial world on the Eastern Fringe. Tyranid invaders from Kraken Hivefleet were held in check by the combined efforts of Space Marines, Imperial Guard and alien Eldar forces.

Being an account of the most celebrated martial achievements of Marneus Calgar, Lord Macragge, Chapter Master of the Ultramarines, each having been proclaimed as a Victorix Maxima within the sacred halls of the Imperial Palace on Ancient Terra.

MARNEUS CALGAR										
	Points	WS	BS	S	T	W	I	A	Ld	Sv
Marneus	168	5	5	4	4	4	5	4	10	2+

Any Ultramarine army that is over 2,000 points in total can be led by Marneus, who counts as one of the HQ choices for the army. He uses the following Wargear and may not be given any additional equipment. He may only be used in a battle where both players have agreed to the use of special characters.

Wargear: *Gauntlets of Ultramar*, frag & krak grenades, Terminator honours (bonus included above), bionics and artificer armour.

SPECIAL RULES

Gauntlets of Ultramar: The *Gauntlets of Ultramar* take the form of a pair of power fists, each with a built-in bolter. The gauntlets are worn as a pair so Marneus receives an extra Attack dice in close combat. The gauntlets' bolters fire together with the same effect as a storm bolter.

Never Falls Back: Marneus never falls back. If called upon to take a Fall Back test he automatically passes it without the dice needing to be rolled. If attacked by a weapon or creature that causes troops to fall back without a test, then the instructions to fall back are ignored. The also applies to any unit led by Marneus.

Independent Character: Unless accompanied by a Command squad, Marneus is an independent character and follows the Independent Character special rules in the Warhammer 40,000 rulebook.

Command Squad: Marneus may be accompanied by a Command squad, see the special entry in the army list. Note that Marneus and his Command squad count as a single HQ choice.

CHIEF LIBRARIAN TIGURIUS OF THE ULTRAMARINES

And so it came to pass that the noble Lord Calgar was approached by Tigurius - most esteemed of his warrior-oracles, who was skilled with shot, blade and farseeing all equally. "Lord Calgar," quoth he. "I had a powerful premonition last eve and dreamed a strange dream, might I share it with you?". The noble Lord Calgar readily agreed, for Tigurius saw much that was hidden to others and gave good advice in all matters. "I saw a beast rise from the depths, a foul abomination so vast in its hunger that it consumed whole worlds. I dreamed I saw the Emperor, crowned in light as he was in the days of the Crusade, bestriding the galaxy. His sword rested upon Macragge". Calgar was greatly troubled by this and asked Tigurius what he thought it meant. Tigurius replied thus. "The Beast rises from the deeps of the void, the Eastern Fringe I believe. The Emperor has appeared directly, indicating that no other help can be expected. The battle shall be at Macragge, so ready all your warriors and your ships and wait."

CHIEF LIBRARIAN TIGURIUS										
	Points	WS	BS	S	T	W	I	A	Ld	Sv
Tigurius	159	5	5	4	4	3	5	4	9	3+

Tigurius may be included in an Ultramarines army and counts as one of its HQ choices. He must be used exactly as described below, and can not be given any additional equipment. He may only be used in a battle where both players have agreed to the use of special characters.

Wargear: *Rod of Tigurius*, *Hood of Hellfire*, bolt pistol, frag & krak grenades, Terminator honours (bonus included above).

SPECIAL RULES

Rod of Tigurius: The *Rod of Tigurius* is a potent force weapon and may be used in the same way as a normal force weapon. It also enables Tigurius to re-roll the dice for a failed Psychic test.

Hood of Hellfire: The *Hood of Hellfire* works in the same way as a normal psychic hood. In addition it doubles the range of Tigurius' *Smite* psychic attack to 24".

Psychic Power – Smite: Tigurius may attempt to use the *Smite* psychic power in his own shooting phase. *Smite* counts as a weapon and hits automatically using the following profile:

Range 12"(24")	Strength 4	Pene 2	Assault 1/Blast

Always an Independent Character: Tigurius is an independent character and follows the Independent Character special rules in the Warhammer 40,000 rulebook. He can not be accompanied by a Command squad.

CAPTAIN CORTEZ OF THE CRIMSON FISTS

CAPTAIN CORTEZ										
	Points	WS	BS	S	T	W	I	A	Ld	Sv
Cortez	116	5	5	4	4	2	5	3	9	3+

You may include Captain Cortez in a Crimson Fists army. If you decide to take him then he counts as one of the HQ choices for the army. He must be used exactly as described below, and may not be given any additional equipment. He can only be used in a battle where both players have agreed to the use of special characters.

Wargear: Bolt pistol, power fist and purity seals.

SPECIAL RULES

Stubborn: Captain Cortez instills a sense of stubborn pride in his men. Ignore the first failed Fall Back test made by a unit in the army. This also applies to things that normally cause a unit to fall back automatically. Note that this ability can only be used once per battle, and must be used the first time a unit has to fall back.

Invulnerable: Cortez carries on fighting no matter what, ignoring wounds that would normally stop even a Space Marine. He is treated as being invulnerable, which means that even if a hit normally ignores all armour saves, Cortez still gets to try and make his saving throw as normal.

Independent Character: Unless accompanied by a Command squad, Cortez is an independent character and follows all the independent character special rules as detailed in the Warhammer 40,000 rulebook.

Command Squad: Cortez may be accompanied by a Command squad, see the special entry in the army list. Note that Cortez & his Command squad count as a single HQ choice.

BLACK TEMPLARS - EMPEROR'S CHAMPION

Upon the eve of glorious battle, it is customary amongst the Imperial Fists and their successors, most notably the Black Templars Chapter, for one among their number to be granted the singular and majestic honour of becoming the Champion of the Emperor. The battle-brethren gather together in prayer to the Emperor and their Primarch, Rogal Dorn. Ecstatic vision will come over one of the assembled brethren and they will be led away by the Company Chaplain to receive the revered vestments of the Champion of the Emperor - the Black Sword, the Armour of Faith and the other numerous accoutrements of the position. The Champion of the Emperor will then spend the following hours until battle is begun in self-meditation and communion with the Emperor. From this he draws great strength, courage and self-assurance, enough to make the Champion seek out the most fell of the Emperor's foes and deal them death in bloody mêlée.

An extract from the Mythos Angelica Mortis (M36), Appendix CXVI "Honorifics of the Legions Astartes."

EMPEROR'S CHAMPION

	Points	WS	BS	S	T	W	I	A	Ld	Sv
Emp. Champion	105	5	4	4	4	2	5	2	9	2+

A Black Templars army may be joined by the Emperor's Champion. If you decide to take him then he counts as one of the HQ choices for the army. He must be used exactly as described below, and may not be given any additional equipment. He can only be used in a battle where both players have agreed to the use of special characters.

Wargear: Artificer armour, Terminator honours (bonus included above), purity seals, iron halo, master-crafted bolt pistol, the *Black Sword*.

SPECIAL RULES

The Black Sword: The *Black Sword* is a potent power weapon and can be used as a single-handed or double-handed weapon. If used as a single-handed weapon it's treated as a power weapon with +1 Strength, and may be used in addition to the Champion's bolt pistol. If used as a double-handed weapon it counts as being the same as a power fist.

Challenge: The Champion may seek out an enemy character and challenge him to single combat. The enemy model must be involved in the same close combat as the Champion, but the two models don't have to be in base contact. A challenge may not be refused. Move the models so they are touching each other and fight out the close combat between them using the normal rules. No other models may attack the Champion or his opponent during a challenge. The outcome of the challenge decides the outcome of the close combat that the Champion and his opponent are involved in; only the wounds they inflict on each other are used when determining which side has won. Note that other models involved in the close combat may fight, it's just that the wounds they inflict are not used for working out the result of the combat.

Always an Independent Character: The Emperor's Champion is always an independent character and follows all the independent character special rules as detailed in the Warhammer 40,000 rulebook. He may not be accompanied by a Command squad.

SALAMANDERS' CHAPLAIN XAVIER

CHAPLAIN XAVIER										
	Points	WS	BS	S	T	W	I	A	Ld	Sv
Xavier	165	5	5	4	4	2	5	4	10	3+

A Salamanders army may be joined by Chaplain Xavier. If you take him then he counts as one of the HQ choices for the army. He must be used exactly as described below, and may not be given any additional equipment. He can only be used in a battle where both players have agreed to the use of special characters.

Wargear: Bolt pistol, crozius arcanum, rosarius, Terminator honours (bonus included above) and *Vulkan's Sigil*.

SPECIAL RULES

Vulkan's Sigil: Lord Vulkan, Primarch of the Salamanders, had a personal icon in the form of a blacksmith's hammer (*"For he smote the Emperor's enemies as a hammer striking an anvil"*). *Vulkan's Sigil* bears this icon and is said to have been carried by the Primarch himself as his badge of office. It is therefore a potent religious artefact for the Salamanders Chapter and counts as a holy relic. It affects all Salamanders Space Marines within 12" when it is revealed, instead of the normal 2D6".

Independent Character: Unless accompanied by a Command squad, Xavier is an independent character and follows the Independent Character special rules in the Warhammer 40,000 rulebook.

Command Squad: Xavier may be accompanied by a Command squad, see the special entry in the army list. Note that Xavier and his Command squad count as a single HQ choice.

> "The faith of the Salamanders is not forged in the chapel, but in the fires of the battlefield."
>
> Chaplain Xavier

SERGEANT LYSANDER, IMPERIAL FISTS VETERAN

VETERAN SERGEANT LYSANDER										
	Points	WS	BS	S	T	W	I	A	Ld	Sv
Lysander	75	4	4	4	4	1	4	2	9	3+

Any Imperial Fist tactical squad can replace its Sergeant for Lysander. He must be used exactly as described below, and may not be given extra equipment. He can only be used in battles where both players have agreed to the use of special characters.

Wargear: Bolter, Terminator honours (bonus included), purity seals, bionics, master-crafted close combat weapon, auspex, frag grenades and krak grenades.

SPECIAL RULES

Bolter Drill: You may re-roll, if you wish, the to hit dice for any bolter fire undertaken by a squad led by Lysander. If you do then you must re-roll all the to hit dice, not just the ones that missed. You may only re-roll bolter fire – bolt pistols and heavy bolters, etc., are not affected by this.

Date: 2455757.M40
Ref: Ecc/8474/BvH2
By: . . . . . . Balthazar van Heppel, Ministorum Envoy
Re: . . . . Report on Adeptus
. . . . Astartes Beliefs
Thought: . . . . Examine your thoughts.

"My first finding was the somewhat uncooperative, some would say purposefully obstructive, nature of the Space Marines. Although given formal commission by the Ecclesiarch himself to investigate the religious practices of the Adeptus Astartes, I have been forced to form most of my conclusions from speculation, hearsay and casual observances. Of the twelve Chapters approached', only three responded directly, and of those the information passed on was cursory and brief in the extreme. However, despite these obstacles, I have formulated a number of preliminary conclusions, as follows.

Like all faithful citizens of the Imperium, the Space Marines give due reverence to the Beneficent Emperor of Mankind. However, here their orthodoxy ends, for it is rumoured that they perpetrate that most unholy of blasphemies and heresies. It is said that they do not worship the Benevolent Emperor as the God he is, but instead give their praise to him only as the founder of the Imperium and their creator. As if this was not heinous enough a crime against His Most Holy Emperor, they commit yet more heresy. Not only do they worship the Emperor, blessèd be He for all eternity, but they also raise their voices in prayer to their Primarchs with equal vigour. They offer up praise for the founding of their Chapter, and the gift of the gene-seed from their Primarch which sustains them.

The manner of this praise takes a different form in every Chapter, although Chapters with a common genealogy will often adhere to similar beliefs and traditions. In many cases, these rites are barbaric in the extreme. Sacrifice is not uncommon in many Chapters, with the warriors proving their martial prowess against various bestial adversaries in bloody combat. The exchange of blood between the Space Marines is also a frequent occurrence, particularly those Chapters which have descended from the original Blood Angels Legion. Captured banners are paraded, the heads of defeated foes exhibited and the manner of their capture or defeat recalled with grim detail and fascination. In all matters religious, the Space Marines emphasise their own prowess and conquests, giving thanks to the Emperor and their Primarch for bestowing them with their martial gifts.

Some Chapters' practices date back from their founding, and are laid upon the foundations of heathen beliefs practised on their home planets. Ritual scarring, tattooing and the daubing of paint on the body are common themes amongst those Chapters which draw their recruits from the semi-civilised worlds of the Imperium. For instance, the Salamanders, raised from the volcanic, ash-laden world of Nocturne, follow the Promethean cult. Offerings are burnt in the sacred fires and intricate, harmonious chants recite the Chapters' achievements, giving praise to the Emperor and Vulkan. Amidst the ruddy glow of the lava flows, they swear allegiance to the Emperor, branding themselves, using red-hot irons, with various symbols of their devotion and victories. The Rampagers, descended from the White Scars Legion who themselves drew upon the nomadic warriors of Mundus Planus, scar themselves in a long ceremony known as the Blooding. Facial scars are a matter of rank and prestige amongst the Rampagers, and the gathered blood from this ritual wounding forms part of the celebration feast that follows.

The beliefs of the Chapter are perpetuated by its Chaplains. These fierce devotees to the Chapter's cult lead the prayers and rituals, and exhort their comrades to acts of valour on the battlefield. I was unable to converse with any Chaplains directly, but they are said to be ferocious individuals; of fiery heart and temperament; quick to anger but also watchful of the souls of their battle brothers. Though the Chaplains are given a miraculous Rosarius to show the bond between them and the Ministorum, it is my belief that any connection between that of their practices and our own noble establishments is faint, if not non-existent."

Investigation of the Religious Beliefs, Rituals and Practices of the Legionnes Astartes. Balthazar van Heppel.

*Angels of Purgatory; Angels of Vigilance; Black Inculpators; Black Templars; Crimson Fists; Flesh Tearers; Imperial Fists; Novamarines; Rampagers; Salamanders; Silver Skulls; Venerators of Osiron.

'1982567.M40. Sergeant Lysander was awarded the Imperial Laurel by Captain Venatus of the Second Company for his acts of extreme courage and resilience under fire. During the righteous pacification of the heretical insurgence on Iduno, Sergeant Lysander bravely led his squad in the stubborn defence of the Colonial Bridge. For fourteen hours, Lysander and his men held against wave after wave of attacks by the hateful rebels who had forsworn the glorious Emperor of Mankind for the False Glories of the Fallen Gods. Well versed in the Rites of Battle, Lysander guided his men surely and strongly, bringing the vengeance of the Emperor in volleys of controlled, effective bolter fire. When Lysander and the survivors of his squad were relieved, it took several hours to clear the corpses of the shadow-shrouded recreants so that the bridge could be crossed.'

Excerpt from the Liber Honorus, Imperial Fists Chapter, Legions Astartes.

SPACE MARINE SCENARIO

SPACE MARINE FORCE

COMPULSORY
1 HQ
2 Troops**

OPTIONAL
1 HQ*
4 Troops**
3 Elites
3 Fast Attack***

*   Characters can not ride bikes.
** Space Marines Assault squads may be taken as Troops in this mission.
*** Only land speeders, land speeder Tornadoes and land speeder Typhoons may be chosen.

HQ

ELITES

TROOPS

TROOPS

FAST ATTACK

DEFENDER'S FORCE

COMPULSORY
1 HQ
1 Elite

OPTIONAL
1 HQ
2 Elites
4 Troops
2 Fast Attack
2 Heavy
Support

HQ

ELITES

TROOPS

TROOPS

FAST ATTACK

HEAVY SUPPORT

The Planetfall mission has the Space Marines making a surgical strike from orbit to take out an enemy HQ. It is a special type of mission and can only be used with your opponent's consent. The Space Marines are always the attackers in this mission.

Use these force organisation charts to work out the forces for this mission (Note that dark toned boxes indicate choices which you **must** include in your army).

The Space Marines fear no Evil for we are Fear Incarnate!

PLANETFALL MISSION

OVERVIEW

Space Marines often carry out special missions that require them to make an assault from an orbiting spacecraft. They are well trained and equipped to carry this out, descending from orbit in huge Thunderhawk gunships or specially designed drop pods, and then unleashing a well-coordinated attack before the enemy knows what hit it.

SCENARIO SPECIAL RULES

Planetfall uses *Deep Strike*, *Hidden Set-Up*, *Victory Points* and *Random Game Length*.

SET-UP

1 The defender sets up using *Hidden Set-Up*, anywhere on the table but at least 12" from a table edge. The defender's hidden set-up is not revealed until after the Space Marines have arrived in their first turn.

2 The Space Marines all enter play on the first turn using the *Deep Strike* rules. Even troops that cannot normally use *Deep Strike* may use it for this mission.

3 The Space Marines get the first turn in this mission.

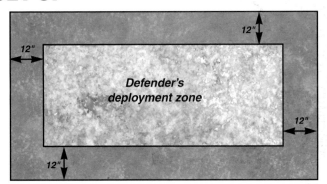

12"

12"

Defender's deployment zone

12"

12"

MISSION OBJECTIVE

The Space Marines must kill all of the defenders' HQ units and score the most victory points. Any other result is a victory for the defenders.

IMPORTANT: The Space Marines score triple the normal number of victory points for HQ units they eliminate in this mission.

RESERVES

None.

GAME LENGTH

The game lasts for a random number of turns (see the Scenario Special Rules on pages 132-137 in the Warhammer 40,000 rulebook).

LINE OF RETREAT

Any unit forced to fall back will head for the nearest table edge using the shortest possible route. The rules for falling back are on pages 71-72 of the Warhammer 40,000 rulebook.

ADEPTUS ASTARTES FLEET CAPABILITIES IN THE GOTHIC SECTOR, OBSCURA SEGMENTUM

27th of Bariel, IR 11,752

Honoured lord, I have instituted the study of Adeptus Astartes naval assets as you requested. My initial findings are below and as you will observe the available information is scant. The Chapter Masters I have contacted have all refused to render detailed information regarding the strength and location of their fleet units, giving only hazy details about individual ship types at best or stony silence at worst. Their repeated implication seems to be that they are more likely to have to fight against Battlefleet Obscura than alongside it, hence their interest in joint fleet operations is minimal.

The majority of the information I have gleaned is from the ships' logs of the Righteous Endeavour and the Demiarch Vespasian, who were both present at the Scylla incident and the subsequent convoy runs through Ork held space. Earlier, well-documented histories are available for the Battle of Macragge and the incursions of the Black Crusade of Vulkarth, but I have found these to be dated and of dubious veracity. I will update this report as I gather more data but the lack of cooperation from the Chapter Masters and the dispersed nature of their forces will be a constant impediment.

ASTARTES SHIP CLASSES

Fortress Monasteries

Several Chapters, most notably the Dark Angels and the Fire Hawks, operate from mobile space fortresses. These gigantic craft contain sufficient accommodation, workshops, training areas and dock facilities for the entire Chapter and operate as a mobile base for Chapter operations. While their defensive/offensive capabilities are alleged to be equivalent to a Ramilies class star fort, they are not only mobile but warp-capable. The warp drives for these structures must be enormous, far exceeding those of our own Emperor class battleships. However the loss of the Fire Hawk's fortress Raptorus Rex during a standard jump from Piraeus to Crow's World in 963 may indicate that these craft are dangerously unstable. Allegedly no Chapter possesses more than a single fortress, on this basis I would estimate that there are between two and five of these behemoths operating in the entire Segmentum, and at most one in the Gothic Sector.

Battle Barges

Battle barges have been reported in conjunction with nearly all major Astartes operations, most recently in the Scylla incident. In this engagement a battle barge of the Harbingers Chapter identified as the Unrelenting Fury intercepted the Scylla and delivered a series of punishing salvoes against it. The Unrelenting Fury was observed to suffer severe engine damage from repeated fighter attacks but was otherwise unharmed.

If the Unrelenting Fury is a typical example of an Astartes main fleet unit the following conclusions can be drawn: As might be expected the vessel is configured for close support of planetary landings and carries numerous bombardment turrets and torpedo tubes. A considerable amount of hull space is given over to launch bays for light intra-system craft and drop pods, observations indicating that up to three companies can be deployed simultaneously.

The vessel is extremely heavily armoured and well shielded, presumably so that it can breach planetary defences without harm coming to its cargo. The Unrelenting Fury was apparently "slow and very stately in its movements" indicating that engine strength is comparatively low in relation to mass, although this may have been due to damage from the fighter attacks. In ship-to-ship combat I would rate this vessel as comparable to an Emperor class battleship, its lower acceleration and closer ranged weapons weighing off against superior armour and shields. Naturally the battle barge would make a frightening opponent in any situation where boarding is involved.

I have been unable to find any definitive information about numbers of battle barges in operation but I have located twenty eight separate reports of incidents involving them in the segmentum over the last 20 years. From these reports I have identified eleven different craft, five appearing in the Gothic sector.

Strike Craft

Strike craft are fast, lightly-armed vessels whose mass is slightly less than our own Dauntless class light cruisers. Their primary function seems to be that of rapid response, reports indicating that they are invariably the first craft to arrive at a threatened planet. Strike craft vary in configuration but share common features of large bays for deploying ordnance and powerful warp engines. Strike craft appear to carry approximately one full company of Space Marines (including support vehicles) and have been observed to deploy them within twenty minutes of arrival in orbit. The sheer numbers of reported sightings of strike craft indicate that they also perform patrol and pursuit functions across a vast area of space. I would estimate that there are approximately one hundred craft of this class operating in the segmentum as a whole, of which twenty to thirty appear in the Gothic sector on a regular basis.

Ordnance

In addition to standard missiles and torpedoes the Adeptus Astartes utilise three main types of ordnance; drop pods, boarding torpedoes and Thunderhawk gunships. Drop pods are basic ablative capsules which descend to a planet in a rapid drop controlled by a ring of retro burners, closely resembling a simple ship's life pod in operation. Drop pod shells examined on Larras Landing show they carry five to ten warriors in exceedingly spartan conditions.

Boarding torpedoes are large self-guiding missiles which appear to carry a similar number of troops and are used for ship to ship boarding actions. The tip of the boarding torpedo contains magnetic clamps, shock absorbers and explosive charges for breaching a target vessel's hull. With both drop pods and boarding torpedoes the troops in transit would be vulnerable during the transport period but detection of these small craft would be very difficult, limiting any defensive measures to the last moments of their approach.

Thunderhawk gunships are employed as intra-system transports moving troops, supplies and ammunition between ships and planets or between planets, moons or asteroids within a star system. Thunderhawks also carry a substantial armament of missiles, rockets and cannon for their size and are used to give direct fire support to the Space Marines once they are on the surface. Though Thunderhawks are relatively ponderous their heavily armoured heat shielding and flexible weaponry make them a prickly proposition when it comes to interception. Most Astartes strike craft appear to carry at least three Gunships, which between them is sufficient to transport a company of Space Marines simultaneously. Battle barges are thought to carry at least nine Thunderhawks each and fortress monasteries might be able to carry thirty or more.

MODUS OPERANDI

Despite their impressive fleet assets the Space Marine's naval assets are primarily directed at transportation, supply and support of ground forces. A typical offensive against a rebel or alien-held planet begins with the arrival of strike craft which engage and clear away defending system ships and may establish a hidden base located within an asteroid field or on a small moon if a protracted campaign is being undertaken. The strike craft then move on to neutralise any orbital defences, ground-based defence laser silos and missile bunkers. Orbital defences are boarded and captured (as occurred on Larras Landing, Bray, Magdelon, Vanaheim and many others) and then turned against ground defences or simply destroyed. Surviving ground defences are sabotaged by scout forces or captured by main force assault troops inserted via drop pods. By preference, if the system defences are weak or still under friendly control, the Space Marines will deploy directly onto the planet's surface, often directly into the midst of a decisive engagement to take advantage of the considerable shock of their arrival.

In addition to the delivery and support of ground forces Astartes vessels will undertake patrol operations to secure a system against pirates or raiders for a limited duration. However they obviously view this as a role which should fall to the Imperial fleet and Chapter Master Verchen of the Iron Fists even went so far as to pass comment on the number of raiders which have recently penetrated the Purgatory system and the blockade around Dudzus.

In conclusion I would surmise that the Adeptus Astartes commands powerful fleet forces, capable of overwhelming even a heavily defended system. In a fleet action they would be at a disadvantage in comparison to Imperial vessels due to their special adaptations for planetary assaults. However it is hard to imagine that the Adeptus Astartes would accept a ship to ship fight on any but the most favourable terms, instead operating against shipping lanes, dock facilities and other vulnerable assets. I only pray that they remain on our side.

Your ob'dt servant,

By the hand of Lord Captain Morley,
attache to the Fleet Insturum of Alien Studies, docking complex Heracles, Cypra Mundi.

APOTHECARY MALUS' TESTIMONY

The four subjects underwent the more rigorous stage 2 and stage 3 analysis and were passed within tolerable limits. Having established the acceptability of the Neophytes, the first stages of gene-processing began.

The primary stages of Zygote implantation, starting with the insertion of the Heart of Guilliman, up to and including the Warrior's Blood[1], proceeded without incident. Development of the implanted organs grew at acceptable rates, without tissue rejection or evidence of pathomitosis. The primary stage of psycho-conditioning was then begun. A standard quad-phase opti-aural inducer stimulates the neural stem to increase consciousness of primary metabolic functions. This works in concert with alchemo-orientation to stabilise catabolism of the gene-seed hormones.

Once acceptance of the first phases was evident, the subjects underwent the secondary phases of Zygote implantation. With the insertion of the Watchful Sleeper[2] psycho-conditioning was increased and chemo-doctrination introduced to certain brain areas to allow for the conscious inducement of the organ's function.

At this stage, Subject A1/9 suffered a transitory relapse. Due to a endochrinal imbalance, the Watchful Sleeper was fluctuating in its functioning, causing the subject to endure a state of uncontrollable semi-consciousness, disorientation and delirium. However, intensive re-doctrination stabilised the condition to the point where corrective surgery of the neural matrix could be completed, alongside a programme of anti-cathartic elixirs. The subject's normal brain processes were restored to within acceptable levels and we proceeded with the implantation of the other Zygotes.

The implantation of the Zygotes up to and including the Killing Bite[3] was entirely successful in three of the subjects. However, Subject B2/1 encountered severe difficulties during the latter stages of muscular development. An unseen discontinuity in the subject's psycho-preparation led to the traumatic failure to release inhibitor genes. Without this counter-measure, the muscular hypertropics invested into the Warrior's Vigour[4] continued to function for a prolonged period, much in excess of that required for full muscular growth.

Unfortunately, this did not become apparent until the hyperactivity of the growth hormone had reached an irreversible stage. Subject B2/1 was removed from further Zygote implantation and kept under increasing physical restraint in the Apothecarion Reclusia to register the subsequent physical traumas and mental imbalances involved in the malfunction.

As the muscle tissue expanded at an exponential rate (a 0.9% growth per day at its height), the internal disparity proved fatal. A Mortis Investus revealed that the torsion pressure induced by the muscle weight was enough to pull apart even the reinforced skeleton and durable internal organs of the subject. Although the extended muscular growth in this case proved fatal, a number of factors made it evident that, within a controlled framework, extraneous muscle growth could prove a worthwhile endeavour, in particular with a view to the creation of more effective assault warriors.

The remaining subjects were implanted with the Quintessence Sacred[5] which will reach maturation during their final training and early missions as Scouts. These Quintessence Sacred, especially that of Subject B1/9 who appears exceptionally talented and will no doubt become a renowned warrior of the Chapter if he survives, will be placed in neo-stasis for the growth of new Zygotes in the future. After their initial term as Initiates within the Tenth Company, the subjects will be ready for insertion of the Emperor's Ward[6] enabling them to interface fully with power armour and complete their training.

Report ends

RECRUITING SERGEANT CASTOR'S TESTIMONY

The subjects were drawn from the nomadic tribes that traverse the Garanda II ash wastes. Recruitment from Garanda II is exceptional in its success (usual induction rate runs at 35% of subjects tested); the warlike lifestyle of the nomads and harsh environment pre-conditions the inhabitants to self-sufficiency, endurance and increased hostility.

Thirty eight indigenous youths were brought to our attention by our Logister Magnus on Garanda II. Of these, twenty seven failed the customary trial by arms and their bodies were buried in the manner of their peoples. The eleven remaining potential Neophytes were subjected to preliminary appraisal and four showed signs of acceptable tolerance levels (age 10–12 Terran years; tissue rejection at 0.5% or less; mental fortitude at 85% or more compatibility). The seven other potentials were rejected at this stage and passed into the care of the Lord of the Household for mental conditioning as Chapter serfs.

CAPTAIN SEPHERA, CHIEF OF RECRUITS' TESTIMONY

After the insertion of the Watchful Sleeper, the subjects began their combat training, which continued as later Zygote implantation, psycho-conditioning and alchemo-doctrination took place. Each admirably dealt with the Rites of the Bolter, the Incantations of Sacrifice and the Litany of Sufferance. Satisfactory assessment on their knowledge of the Rites of Battle Drill established the Chapter's basic combat requirements.

Power armour simulation was undertaken with tolerable skill, in particular Subject B1/9 showed above average competence and was put through an advanced training program with the intention of incorporating the Doctrines of Assault during his period with the Tenth Company. All four subjects showed rapid adaptation to the stimulation of the newly imposed Zygotes within a combat situation, reacting well to injury and battle-strain as befits the Warriors of the Silver Skulls. Until his internment in the Apothecarion, subject B2/1 showed the potential to become a fine warrior, always eager for combat practice and never tardy in the resolution of his duties.

CHAPLAIN DEIAD'S TESTIMONY

The subjects were given doctrinal awareness in accordance with the rituals and ceremonies of our Chapter. The subjects have proved highly devotional to the Chapter and the Great Emperor of Man. Their knowledge of the Orthodoxy of Varsavia and the Dedications to Terra is complete. They can recite the first eighteen verses of the Book of Victory as would be expected of brethren their age. The three surviving Neophytes all successfully completed the Ascension Fasting, the Deliberation of Spirit and the Initiate Doctoris to be welcomed as Initiates within the Chapter's battle brothers. They have shown the necessary commitment to their battle brothers in combat-stress appraisals and have displayed admirable courage and determination. In particular, they behaved with admirable respect and due reverence during the Attendance to the Departed, each intoning the Prayer to the Departed without hesitation or self-conscious restraint. In all respects, truly worthy Protectors of the Emperor.

DIRECTED TO:	Magios Biologis Benedixta
TRANSMITTED:	Varsavia
RECEIVED:	Kiropadist
TELEPATHIC DUCT:	Astropath-terminus Gebri
DATE:	7185934.M40
PENNED BY:	Jordon Salvus, Lord of the Household, Legions Astartes Silver Skulls
TRANSLATED BY:	Bekonnen Feist, Divisio Dialecta
THOUGHT: Destroy the Impure	

1) Phase 1: Secondary Heart to Phase 5: Larramans Organ.
2) Phase 6: Catalepsean Node - the organ which allows a Space Marine to rest whilst retaining full sensory coherence.
3) Phase 17: Betchers Gland - introduces a poisonous, semi-acidic compound to the saliva.
4) Phase 3: Biscopea - inserted in the first year of preparation to promote muscle growth.
5) Phase 18: Progenoid Organs - the repository of the Neophyte's gene-seed which must be re-collected and stored to grow Zygotes for future Neophytes.
6) Phase 19: Black Carapace.

STRATEGIC DISPOSITION OF THE ULTRAMARINES CHAPTER (6500745.M41)

As requested, here is the organisational arrangement of the Ultramarines Chapter of the Legions Astartes, at date shown (note that vehicles (not bikes) and spacecraft include complete crew complements). Current major commitments of military resources shown in Addenda 1.

Compiled by Lorex Vanidius, Assimilator Major, Treaty of Macragge Inspectorate.

We are the inheritors of Roboute. Let no rule be beyond us. Let no man stand in our way.

HEADQUARTERS

Marneus Calgar,
Lord Macragge,
Master of the Ultramarines

Ancient Helveticus,
Chapter Standard Bearer

3 Chaplains, 3 Rhinos,
2 Land Raiders, 5 Razorbacks
206 Non Space Marine support and administrative staff
(inc. Masters Secretarius, Lord of the Household, Equerry Primus, Master of the Sanctum, Regulator Primus & 12 Astropaths)

FLEET COMMAND

48 Pilots, Gunnery Officers & Command Crews,
18 Navigators,
8 Strike Cruisers,
3 Battle Barges – *Octavius, Caesar, Severian,*
12 Rapid Strike vessels,
32 Thunderhawks

LIBRARIUS

Chief Librarian Tigurius
4 Epistolaries, 7 Codiciers,
12 Lexicaniums, 4 Acolytum

ARMOURY

Fennias Maxim, Master of the Forge
4 Techmarines Suprema, 28 Techmarines,
8 Apprenta, 103 Servitors, 72 Techno-mats,
14 Predator Destructors,
11 Predator Annihilators, 8 Vindicators,
9 Whirlwinds, 14 Rhinos, 14 Razorbacks,
12 Land Raiders (including variants)

APOTHECARION

Corpus Helix, Chief Apothecary,
11 Apothecaries, 5 Initiates, 31 Servo-meds

℧ BATTLE COMPANIES ℧

FIRST COMPANY

Captain Invictus, Regent of Ultramar,
Magister Primus,
2 Chaplains,
1 Apothecary,
1 Company Standard Bearer,
8 Veteran Sergeants,
87 Veteran Space Marines,
74 Tactical Dreadnought suits,
3 Dreadnoughts,
18 Rhinos,
7 Land Raiders

SECOND COMPANY

Captain Agemman, Commander of the Watch
1 Chaplain, 1 Apothecary,
1 Co. Standard Bearer, 2 Veteran Sergeants,
5x10-strong Tactical squads,
1x8-strong Tactical squad,
1x10-strong Assault squad,
1x9-strong Assault squad,
2x10-strong Devastator squads,
2 Dreadnoughts,
11 Rhinos, 3 Land Speeders,
2 Land Speeder Tornadoes,
1 Land Speeder Typhoon,
18 Bikes, 2 Attack Bikes

Note: 2nd Battle Company presently mobilised on Talassar to respond to immediate requirements.

THIRD COMPANY

Captain Ardias, Commander of the Arsenal
1 Chaplain, 1 Apothecary,
1 Co. Standard Bearer, 3 Veteran Sergeants,
6x10-strong Tactical squads,
1x8-strong Assault squad,
1x5-strong Assault squad,
2x10-strong Devastator squads,
2 Dreadnoughts,
9 Rhinos, 2 Land Speeders,
2 Land Speeder Tornadoes,
3 Land Speeder Typhoons,
20 Bikes, 4 Attack Bikes

Note: Majority of 3rd Company in transit to Joran VI.

FOURTH COMPANY

Captain Idaeus, Commander of the Fleet
1 Chaplain, 1 Apothecary,
1 Company Standard Bearer,
5 Veteran Sergeants,
6x10-strong Tactical squads,
2x10-strong Assault squads,
2x10-strong Devastator squads,
4 Dreadnoughts,
15 Rhinos, 5 Land Speeders,
5 Land Speeder Tornadoes,
5 Land Speeder Typhoons,
25 Bikes, 5 Attack Bikes

Notes: 4th Company now at full combat strength.

FIFTH COMPANY

Captain Sicarius, Master of the Marches
1 Apothecary,
1 Co. Standard Bearer, 1 Veteran Sergeant,
3x10-strong Tactical squads,
2x6-strong Tactical squads,
1x5-strong Tactical squad,
1x9-strong Assault squad,
1x6-strong Assault squad,
1x9-strong Devastator squad,
1x5-strong Devastator squad,
1 Dreadnought, 7 Rhinos, 4 Land Speeders,
1 Land Speeder Typhoon, 12 Bikes, 1 Attack Bike

Notes: 5th Company suffered heavy losses during Barchi Scouring (6342745.M41). Requires new Chaplain and reorganisation of squads.

℧ RESERVE COMPANIES ℧

SIXTH COMPANY

Captain Epathus
1 Chaplain,
1 Apothecary,
1 Company Standard Bearer,
4 Veteran Sergeants,
6x10-strong Tactical squads,
3x8-strong Tactical squads,
1x5-strong Tactical squad,
4 Dreadnoughts, 13 Rhinos,
21 Bikes, 3 Attack Bikes

SEVENTH COMPANY

Captain Ixion, Chief Victualler
1 Chaplain, 1 Apothecary,
1 Co. Standard Bearer, 2 Veteran Sergeants,
8x10-strong Tactical squads,
1x9-strong Assault squad,
1x6-strong Tactical squad,
3 Dreadnoughts, 15 Rhinos,
4 Land Speeders, 3 Land Speeder Tornadoes,
4 Land Speeder Typhoons

Note: 7th Company serving as Master Guards on Caeser.

EIGHTH COMPANY

Captain Numitor
1 Chaplain, 1 Apothecary,
1 Co. Standard Bearer, 3 Veteran Sergeants,
7x10-strong Assault squads,
3x8-strong Assault squads,
5 Dreadnoughts, 16 Rhinos,
28 Bikes, 7 Attack Bikes,
8 Land Speeders, 4 Land Speeder Tornadoes,
5 Land Speeder Typhoons

Note: Majority of 8th Company on extended combat training on Gava II

NINTH COMPANY

Captain Sinon
1 Chaplain, 1 Apothecary,
1 Company Standard Bearer,
2 Veteran Sergeants,
6x10-strong Devastator squads,
1x9-strong Devastator squad,
2x6-strong Devastator squad,
1x5-strong Devastator squad,
7 Dreadnoughts,
8 Rhinos

TENTH COMPANY

Captain Antilochus, Chief of Recruits
1 Chaplain, 1 Apothecary,
3 Veteran Sergeants,
2x10-strong Scout squads,
2x8-strong Scout squads,
3x6-strong Scout squads,
5x5-strong Scout squads,
7 Recruiting Sergeants, 17 Neophytes
*Notes: Neophyte survival at 54%.
Last recruitment Copul VI, 6 accepted*

℧ VETERANS ℧

℧ SCOUTS ℧

ADDENDA 1

COUNTER-INCURSION – GERIO SECTOR

Armoury – 2 Predator Annihilators, 1 Vindicator, 1 Razorback, 2 Techmarines, 4 Servitors
Librarius – 1 Epistolary, 1 Apothecarion – 3 Servo-meds
Fleet – 1 Strike Cruiser – Emperor's Mercy, 3 Thunderhawks
1st Company – 5 Terminators
6th Company – Captain, Apothecary, Co. Standard Bearer, 2 Veteran Sergeants,
15 Tactical Space Marines, 1 Dreadnought, 1 Rhino, 2 Land Speeders, 5 Bikes, 1 Attack Bike.
8th Company – 20 Assault Space Marines
9th Company – 5 Devastator Space Marines
10th Company – 5 Scouts
Majority of Chapter engaged in routine patrol sweeps
of Ultramar and surrounding sectors, as per Treaty of Macragge.

PROTECTION FORCE – EXPLORATOR FLEET DELPHA

Armoury – 2 Techmarines, 6 Servitors
Librarius – 1 Epistolary Apothecarion – 1 Apothecary, 5 Servo-meds
Fleet – 3 Thunderhawks
1st Company – 5 Terminators
4th Company – Captain, Chaplain, Apothecary, 2 Veteran Sergeants,
30 Tactical Space Marines, 1 Dreadnought, 1 Rhino, 2 Land Raiders
10th Company – 5 Scouts
Additional: Under nominal command of Rogue Trader Santez Knave. Battle
command still resides with Captain Idaeus

JORAN VI RETALIATION FORCE

Armoury – 4 Predator 'Annihilators', 6 Predator 'Destructors', 6 Razorbacks, 3 Land Raiders,
4 Vindicators, 9 Whirlwinds, 5 Rhinos, 5 Techmarines, 18 Servitors
Librarius – 3 Lexicaniums, 1 Codicier
Apothecarion – 1 Apothecary, 10 Servo-meds
Fleet – 2 Strike Cruisers – Fist of Ultramar, Righteous Fury; 12 Thunderhawks
1st Company – 10 Veterans, 1 Rhino
3rd Company – Captain, Chaplain, Apothecary, Company Standard Bearer, 1 Veteran Sergeant,
35 Tactical Space Marines, 20 Devastator Space Marines, 8 Assault Space Marines, 2
Dreadnoughts, 6 Rhinos, 6 Land Speeders (2 Tornadoes, 2 Typhoons), 10 Bikes, 2 Attack Bikes
10th Company – 20 Scouts
Additional: Due to combine with Imperial Guard Regiments – Joran XV, Belios IV and Yama XXV

LEGION	PRIMARCH	WORLD	SECOND FOUNDING CHAPTERS
Dark Angels	Lion El' Jonson	[Caliban]	Angels of Absolution, Angels of Redemption, Angels of Vengeance
All records expunged from library - order origination unknown			
Emperor's Children	Fulgrim	[Chemos]	Excommunicate Traitoris
Iron Warriors	Perturabo	[Olympia]	Excommunicate Traitoris
White Scars	Jaghatai Khan	Mundus Planus	Marauders, Rampagers, Destroyers, Storm Lords
Space Wolves	Leman Russ	Fenris	Wolf Brothers
Imperial Fists	Rogal Dorn	Terra	Black Templars, Crimson Fists
Night Lords	Konrad Curze	[Nostramo]	Excommunicate Traitoris
Blood Angels	Sanguinius	Baal	Angels Encarmine, Angels Sanguine, Angels Vermilion, Blood Drinkers, Fleshtearers
Iron Hands	Ferrus Manus	Medusa	Red Talons; Brazen Claws
All records expunged from library - order origination unknown			
Worldeaters	Angron	No Record	Excommunicate Traitoris
Ultramarines	Roboute Guilliman	Macragge	Novamarines, Patriarchs of Ulixis, White Consuls, Black Consuls, Libators, Inceptors, Praetors of Orpheus, Genesis Chapter
Death Guard	Mortarion	[Barbarus]	Excommunicate Traitoris
Thousand Sons	Magnus the Red	[Prospero]	Excommunicate Traitoris
Lunar Wolves	Horus	[Cthonia]	Excommunicate Traitoris
Word Bearers	Lorgar	[Colchis]	Excommunicate Traitoris
Salamanders	Vulkan	Nocturne	None Known
Raven Guard	Corax	Deliverance	Black Guard, Revilers, Raptors
Alpha Legion	Alpharius	No Record	Excommunicate Traitoris

Dark Angels

For reasons undisclosed, the Dark Angels and their Second Founding successors refer to themselves as the Unforgiven.
Source: Mythos Angelica Mortis (M.36)

Space Wolves

"The Space Wolves encourage genetic deviancy [re: extraordinary growth of canines] and show extreme unorthodoxy in their tactics and organisation."
Source: Personal Comment Inquisitor Horst (M.37)

Blood Angels

Charge: Blood Angels and their successors follow unconventional and deviant gene-replication practices which has led to the debasement of their gene-seed.

Comment: Rumours of 'Red Thirst' and 'Black Rage' still perpetuate, despite investigation on numerous occasions.
Source: Authorised Report - Inquisitor Damne (M.34)

Ultramarines

These are the named Successors to the Ultramarines Legion (Apocrypha of Davio), though the Apocrypha of Skaros states there are 23 Second Founding Chapters but fails to name them.
Source: Compiler Atreax (M.41)

Ultramarines

The Ultramarines Legion is responsible for nearly 3/5ths of the gene-core of the current Space Marine Chapters. The Ultramarines Chapter rules large empire in Galactic South-East, known as Ultramar, one of the most powerful institutions on the Eastern Fringe.
Source: Liber Astartes (M.37)

Lunar Wolves

The Lunar Wolves were renamed Sons of Horus (c.125.M30). After the death of Horus, they became known as the Black Legion.
Source: Grimoire Hereticus (M.35)

LEGION: Name of Legion when founded.
PRIMARCH: Name of Primarch from which Legion allegedly drew its geneseed.
WORLD: Where Legion was based. Worlds in parentheses subsequently destroyed.

SECOND FOUNDING CHAPTERS - Chapters named in Apocrypha of Davio [M.33].
EXCOMMUNICATE TRAITORIS - Those Legions who turned during the Great Heresy as reported in the Grimoire Hereticus [M.35]

Ultramar & the surrounding systems
Archive: Librarium Cartographia, Mars III (M.40)
-57

-30 M31 The **Great Heresy**, nearly half of the Space Marine Legions turn on the Emperor and follow **Horus**. Horus is defeated and the **Traitor Legions** are driven into the **Eye of Terror**.

-32 M31 **Roboute Guilliman**, Primarch of the Ultramarines Legion, compiles the first **Codex Astartes**. This volume lays down new organisational doctrine.

C.M29 The **Primarchs** are developed, supposedly twenty in number. An unknown disaster scatters them across galaxy before fully grown.

Loyal Space Marine Legions are broken down into smaller Chapters, each numbering roughly 1,000 fighting troops. One Chapter retains name and heraldry of Legion, other Chapters re-named and given new icons and uniforms as detailed in Codex Astartes. This is known as the **Second Founding**.

"Primarchs - early attempt to use gene-alteration to create humans with godlike power"
Liber Historica vangelia [M.34]

C.M25 **Horiax Treatise** mentions genetic alteration techniques

-34

60 | M25 | M26 | M27 | M28 | M29 | M30 | M31 | M32 |

-35

C.M28 Earliest modified warriors aid the Emperor in conquest of Terra.

M32+ The Primarchs reportedly die or disappear over the following millennia. Through subsequent Foundings, the number of Space Marine Chapters is increased.

M29 The **Great Crusade** begins. Each of the Primarchs rediscovered on human worlds, invariably having risen to positions of power due to their ultra-enhanced minds and bodies.

Known Chapters at present: 989-1021*
*See Files re: Badoon War, Jasepak Scouring, Fall of Joq

M30 **Grabya's Theorem** demonstrates how Primarch genetic data could have b used to stabilise genetic development of new Space Marines. Twenty F **Founding** Space Marine Legions are formed, each led by one of the Primarchs

Chapter Losses [765.M41]	
Lost in Warp	13
Irrecoverable Battle Losses	21
Gene-seed failure	9
Inquisitorial Purge	4
Other Circumstances	16

-37

M30 Great Crusade continues. Sorian's **Inductus Excelsus** shows requirements for more warriors is vast. Accelerated gene-culturing techniques implemented, reducing processing time to create a Space Marine to a single year. Accelerated gene-seed has unseen fundamental flaws.

-39

Archive: Taken from engraving, Tomb of the Saviour, Bellis Argent (M.31)

Ref: 3526/b
Date: 2384646.M40
File: Ultra/3a
Status: Sealed data
Relay: Sectum 34
Access: I/A/AA

The Emperor knows, the Emperor is watching

PLATE IX LEGIONS ASTARTES - FOUNDING HISTORY (ref.903.33 & Mal.940a).

"Consider the Predator.
Let your soul
be armoured with Faith,
driven on the tracks of
Obedience which overcomes all
obstacles,
and armed with the three great
guns of Zeal, Duty and Purity."

Anon.

LEGIONES ASTARTES DAILY RITUALS

0400 Morning Prayer. Day is begun with morning prayer and contemplation within the Company Chapel, led by the Company Chaplain. The Company standard and relics are displayed and the brethren repeat their oaths of loyalty to the Chapter and the Emperor. At this juncture the Captain may choose to address the brethren, issue orders, make any appropriate announcements (such as awards and promotions) and dispense summary punishments as deemed necessary.

0500 Morning Firing Rites. After prayer is complete the brethren undertake the first firing rites of the day. A variety of weaponry is used but the emphasis is placed on practice with the Space Marine's personal weaponry. Awards are made for consistently good marksmanship and punishments are inflicted for poor weapon discipline and accuracy. The firing rites may be undertaken in the ranges located in the armoury or outside the fortress.

0700 Battle Practice. The first battle practice of the day is generally geared towards hand-to-hand combat and close quarter fighting. The exact procedures followed vary immensely but often include numerous live-firing exercises and simulated battle conditions in a number of lethal or near-lethal environments. For this reason (and for reasons of defence) most of the Space Marine fortress monasteries are often situated in extremely inhospitable areas be they arctic, volcanic, corrosive, swamp, carnivorous jungle or a combination thereof.

1200 Midday Prayer. The brethren are gathered once more to give praise to the Emperor and their Primarch. During extended battle practice such prayer may be undertaken in the field, potentially while live-firing exercises continue. At this time any brethren severely injured in the morning battle practice are transported to the Apothecarion.

1300 Midday Meal. The Space Marines partake of their first sustenance of the day at this juncture. Frequently this will be a substance inedible to ordinary humans or a local lifeform which is hunted and slain during the morning battle practice.

1315 Tactical indoctrination. Hypnotherapy and psycho-conditioning are used to rapidly assimilate the Chapter tactical doctrines on a number of subjects. New battle languages are learned, alien weaponry, troops and vehicles are studied. Squad and company tactics are reviewed and lessons learned from the morning battle practice are examined.

1500 Battle Practice. Afternoon battle practice usually revolves around squad and company level tactics and reinforcement of the tactical indoctrination segment. Specialist squads such as devastators and assault troops will often use this opportunity to hone their particular skills while the tactical brethren practice close support with Dreadnoughts, armour and personnel carriers.

2000 Evening prayer. Evening prayer is viewed as a time for contemplation and giving thanks for the day's lessons learned. Once more praise is rendered to the Emperor and the Chapter's Primarch for the inception and existence of the Chapter. Gene-seed sampling may be undertaken at this time as it has by now been fully stimulated by the day's activities.

2100 Evening meal. The evening meal is a more sedate affair than that at midday, with a substantial repast provided by the Chapters serf's under the watchful eye of the Lord of the Household. Substantial quantities of protein rich food are made available, particularly to the younger brethren. Indulgent Chapter Masters may even permit the brethren to partake of alcoholic beverages at this time if the day's activities have been expertly done.

2130 Night Fighting Exercises. Chapters based on worlds where there is no perceptible night segment, or on ships in the void use this opportunity to practice combat underwater, in zero gravity, through dense fog or smoke or in other exotic conditions.

2315 Maintenance Rituals. Each Space Marine is expected to maintain and repair his own armour and weaponry according to standard rituals. Seriously damaged or defective gear is surrendered to the Master of the Forge for inspection and repair. Every effort is made to ensure that a Space Marine keeps the same set of equipment after their investiture so that they develop a close bond and understanding of the machine spirits they will rely on in battle.

2345 Free time. Some Chapter Masters view this period of free time as an unwarranted luxury at best and a dangerous distraction at worst. It is maintained in most Chapters out of reverence for the Codex Astartes and Roboute Guilliman's words. "Consider (the) magnitude of your duty at your leisure, but act without hesitation when (action) is required". In honour of this Space Marines are permitted a short period of leisure each day to consider the magnitude of their duty to the Emperor.

0000 Rest Period Begins. Space Marines do not truly need sleep thanks to the Catalepsean Node - an implant in their brain that enables them to rest half of their brain at a time whilst still maintaining awareness with the other half. However extended interference with the circadian rhythms of sleep has been shown to impair efficiency and induce personality disorders. To prevent this Space Marines enter a dreamless fugue state for four hours per day when not on campaign. The longest recorded incident of a Space Marine unit going without sleep was during the Rynn's World incident (Ref. 061.24/A) when the Crimson Fists remnants led by Master Kantor remained operational for a period of 328.7 standard hours.

Notes::

Many Chapter Masters and Company Captains favour changing times and details of the daily ritual to keep their brethren alert and able to quickly assimilate new orders or situations. Interruption of the rest period is frequent and the elimination of meals and the shortening of prayer times commonplace.

All Chapters have high days or feast days which usually celebrate the ascendance of the Emperor to the Golden Throne and the birth and death of their own Primarch (the actual dates observed for these practices vary immensely). On such special days all members of the Chapter who are present at the fortress will gather in the Assimularum for prayers led by the Chapter Master followed by a day long celebration which traditionally includes contests of skill and strength. This is also the traditional time for the acceptance of Neophytes, the elevation of Neophytes to initiates, and the elevation of Initiates to Full Brethren. When there are worthy candidates, brethren may also be accepted into the Veteran company on a feast day. In all cases trials by ordeal are common, and in some cases fatal.

Typically Brethren with special skills are permitted to work in the forges or the Apothecarion between the evening meal and rest period at the discretion of the Company Captain. There they are taught by the Tech-Marines or Apothecaries in their arcane crafts. Exceptional artisans and chirurgeons will be elevated to apprentice Techmarines or Apothecaries after a suitable period spent in vigil within the Solitorium.

The honour of guarding the Chapter Fortress is generally rotated between the 1st through 5th Companies according to which are present at the time. The 6th through 9th (reserve) companies train more regularly as they bear the majority of the Chapters most recently inducted brethren.

Brethren undertake penitence and purgation if they fail in their duties. This is usually self-imposed as a mark of dedication to the Emperor. Gross breaches of Chapter law may be met with death or exile of permanent or temporary nature (temporary exile is usually linked to the achievement of a specified goal).

Compiled from information supplied by the Black Consuls, Salamanders, Fleshtearers, Ultramarines and Silver Skulls Chapters. Additional notes are culled from the Codex Astartes (M38 transcription) and personal commentary by Captain Alhaus of the Black Templars.